The Boomer's Guide to Aging Parents: The Complete Guide, Carolyn Rosenblatt, R.N., Attorney at Law.

This information and advice published or made available in this book is not intended to replace the services of a physician, attorney or any other professional or government organization.

The author and publisher make no representations or warranties with respect to any information offered or provided in this book regarding effectiveness, action or application of the protocols contained herein. The author and publisher are not liable for any loss or damage, direct or indirect, resulting from use of the information contained here.

Table of Contents

Introduction

This book did not start out to be a book. It started with people asking questions. I retired from my litigation practice in 2007, after 29 years on the legal battlefield, as a litigator and trial lawyer. I had already taken several kinds of mediation training, and was beginning to do mediations. Sometimes people had a conflict, which needed dispute resolution services, but more often, they had questions about aging parents and relatives.

I had set out to do mediation (dispute resolution) for elders in elder care facilities, or wherever they were, so my focus was already on elders. I found myself answering questions more than mediating. It was interesting that so many questions were about the law, and how it interfaced with the healthcare issues of aging loved ones: elder abuse, assisted living facilities, contracts, family fights, who should take care of mom, and lots of other issues that were generating questions from clients and their families.

As a result, my consulting practice was born. What is satisfying for me is being able to use both nursing knowledge and legal knowledge in the same conversation with a client. It took eight years to get both of those degrees and many more years to get enough experience in both fields to be able to figure out what people needed to know. I feel deeply honored to be able to use the combined forty years of experience I have to be of assistance to anyone.

What I have observed is that people who are caring for aging parents do not face just one problem with those parents. Aging brings with it multiple problems for the caregivers. Some are health related. Some are emotional. Some are legal. Some are a combination. Usually, they are all mixed together in some way. My background seemed like a very good fit to be of service to those doing the sometimes very difficult job of caregiver.

I work with my husband, Dr. Mikol Davis, a clinical psychologist with over thirty years' experience, in consulting work and mediations. Particularly in working with families in conflict, his input is invaluable. He encouraged me to write things down, as so much helpful information comes from our clients. The writing seemed to grow and grow. Before I knew it, one chapter led to another, until there were nine, with more to come.

My hope is that this book will relieve a little pressure, bring a little clarity, give some practical, hands-on advice, and help you, to have a better understanding of how the law, knowledge about the healthcare system, and common sense can help you get through this time. My husband and I are baby boomers, too. For all of us, this caretaking time is a new era in our lives. My wish for you is that you feel some support from your fellow boomer author.

Carolyn L. Rosenblatt, R. N., Attorney at Law

Acknowledgments

No book can be written without inspiration from someone or something. This one is inspired by many.

Perhaps my love of being around older persons was first inspired by my wonderful grandmother, who lived her life to the fullest, staying in her home through all her declining years, until her death at age 93. She was an observer of people, and taught me to be the same, and to value what was unique in each one. Thank you, Mimi.

As a student nurse, I worked in a nursing home situated next to the nurses' dorm. It was there that I first worked with groups of aging folks. When I needed some money, I could take a shift on the weekend, and there was always work at the nursing home. I liked the work. Summers, before obtaining my license, it was the same. There was always a job available working with elders. I spent time caring for aging persons at home, in long-term care, and in the hospital where we got most of our training.

As a young public health nurse assigned to visit my clients at their homes, I discovered that I was going to be assigned a lot of "geriatrics" patients. I didn't know what to think. However, I went at it with enthusiasm. I was amazed to find out how much I enjoyed working with elders and seeing them in their own environment, rather than hospitals. The interest they had in my visits, the gratitude they showed me for the simplest thing, the true connection we made as I cared for them was a profound experience. I was fascinated, as well as inspired by how they managed, no matter what they had to overcome.

When I finally left nursing to become a lawyer (in significant part because of the limited income nurses made in those days), I left with a tear in my eye. I knew I would miss the twinkling eyes of my older folks, the smiles they gave me each home visit, and the wrinkled hands, gnarled fingers, canes, glasses, dentures and all. There was something touching about all that for me. I could never explain it exactly. I just felt at home with elders.

I acknowledge all those clients, through thousands of visits, thousands of hands I held, countless treatments I gave them, for the lessons they taught me. I am a wiser person for all the bits of wisdom they offered. Some had only one leg, some were blind, some could not speak, some had dementia, some were dying and did die, and some were just very old and frail. This book is, in part, a tribute to each and every one of them, and their families, whom I also knew. They taught me more than I could ever express.

Throughout my legal career, in which I nearly always represented injured people, I saw hundreds of clients in hundreds of difficult circumstances. Many suffered; many were disabled for a time or for good. I witnessed another dimension of human courage by being in their lives. I learned volumes from them, too. They gave me the opportunity to really see what it was like to be deprived of a way to make a living because of a disabling injury.

My job included dealing with every kind of insurance, including Medicare, Medicaid, supplemental, health, auto and disability. I learned more from those cases than I ever could have known as a nurse. I saw how hard it was for people to manage insurance problems without an advocate. I had to get evidence for and prove such intangibles as suffering, emotional injury, and partial disability. I had to delve into and articulate what it was like for the person who had lost function in a part of himself. I came to a much deeper understanding of people's lives when I had to learn so much about them, in order to effectively represent them, and to speak for them.

I dedicate this book to the many wonderful clients I served as a personal injury lawyer, as well as the patients and clients I served as a nurse. Touching their lives was a privilege that gave me another dimension. They were and are my teachers. The lessons they taught me permit me to keep helping others who are struggling with problems associated with aging. A host of friends and colleagues helped me get this book project finished. My thanks to my fellow attorney in elder law, Eliot Lippman, Esq., who was a chapter reviewer, along with other chapter reviewers Tina Cheplick, R.N., Franza Giffen, fiduciary, Erin Winter, home care professional, and Michele Budinot, care manager. My amazing assistant Rosemarie Doherty helped me with everything, including research, and all of the mechanical aspects of production. I truly could not have done this without their help.

Finally, my thanks goes to my outstanding husband, Dr. Mikol Davis, psychologist, support team, new work partner at AgingParents.com, and patient listening ear for the last 27 years. I have the gift of a "low maintenance" husband! He is my dearest friend and beacon of light, always.

Carolyn L. Rosenblatt

Chapter One
How to Handle a Dangerous Older Driver

Introduction

This is the first chapter is dedicated to helping boomers with the problems they face with their aging parents. Driving is sometimes a pressing issue. Adult children may feel very stressed in trying to talk about it with their aging loved ones, as most people don't like the idea of giving up their right to drive.

When we learn to drive, we never get a course that tells us how long we're safe to drive. Community programs for older driver safety emphasize keeping older people safer by updating their driving skills and providing refresher information about safe driving. No one gives us a clear idea of the end point for safe driving.

This chapter is for those adult children who believe that Mom or Dad, or perhaps a grandparent, has become a dangerous driver. If you're not sure how to tackle the subject, I hope you'll find some solutions here. If you've already tried to talk about it, and been rejected, this chapter is for you.

I urge you to take action if you already know your aging loved one is no longer safe behind the wheel. Other people need you to do this, before something terrible happens. There may be many ways to go about approaching the subject of taking away the car keys. This chapter offers my own personal plan to make the job easier. It's based on years of representing victims of accidents, some caused by older drivers who never should have been allowed behind the wheel. When it comes to deciding if the dangerous aging person is okay to drive, please consider it your responsibility. The world will thank you.

How to Handle a Dangerous Older Driver

No one wants to think about getting old, much less having to give up driving. If you have an aging loved one and are worried about his safety when he gets behind the wheel, it's time to take action. Planning what to do is a process and it should never be taken lightly. The impact of losing the ability and right to drive can be very devastating and life changing.

Addressing the subject of whether or not your aging loved one should give up the car keys is tricky at best, and emotionally harrowing at worst. A few open minded and flexible people actually choose to give up driving on their own, without being asked. However, most aging adults who become impaired drivers do not recognize it themselves. It's only human for them to avoid the subject, or deny it, if it is pointed out.

Most of us love freedom and independence and the car is symbolic of total freedom. No one wants to lose freedom, so we can expect that elders will cling fast to the idea that they are just fine, regardless of what anyone else thinks. Control is very important to most of us, and as people age, the issue of control becomes a source of anxiety and fear for some. Loss of control of anything that symbolizes independence can be a "hot button" issue, and the right to drive is near the top of the list of things over which a person would not want to lose control.

The subject of older drivers and safety is one with which I have extensive personal experience. For nearly three decades, I handled hundreds of injury cases, representing victims who were injured in auto accidents. In cases in which the accident was caused by an elder, who likely should not have been driving, the situation was usually the same. The elder had no recollection of the accident or did not know what happened. This occurred even when both vehicles were destroyed beyond repair in the collision, the elder had run someone off the road, had run a red light, or caused another such memorable crash.

In one case in which the elder had rear-ended the victim and pushed her car off the road and into a tree, he testified that the other driver had come at him and backed her car into his. Of course, this was impossible, given the position in which the police found both cars. His front bumper was smashed into her rear bumper and she was pinned to the tree by his car. The elder was so confused he literally did not know what he had done. Being confronted with the circumstances of the accident, as happened in a lawsuit, was just too much to face. He could not confront the fact that his driving had caused a crash, so he invented a bizarre explanation.

For aging persons with impaired thinking, this is not an unusual scenario. Memory lapses, slowed reaction time, vision trouble, hearing loss, confusion and other age-related thinking problems all contribute to the dangers of some elder drivers being on the road. News reports of multiple deaths caused by an unsafe older driver are sobering. In one such news report, an elder driver stepped on the gas instead of the brake, causing death and injuries. In his confusion, he stated he "lost control" of the car for reasons unknown. There is always something that cannot be explained, because the driver is unable to say what happened.

A 2006 study by the Insurance Institute for Highway Safety found that only teen drivers have a higher rate of fatal crashes than drivers aged 65 and over, based on number of miles driven.[1] In 2003, 86-year old George Weller killed 10 people and injured 63 others at a street market in southern California, driving through "road closed" signs and wooden barriers. He showed no remorse when sentenced to five year's probation on ten counts of vehicular manslaughter. Driving tragedies involving dangerous older drivers, resulting in injury or death, could be a risk for one of your own parents. The injured or killed could be your family members.

Some older drivers are perfectly safe. They drive safely well into their 80s, or even 90s and beyond. Getting older does not automatically mean that one is an unsafe driver, as each person ages differently. Many older drivers, with long years of driving experience, manage well behind the wheel and are more careful than younger drivers. However, not all older drivers are so lucky as to drive well until the end of their days. According to the Insurance

---

[1] Derocher, Robert J., "Licensing Older Drivers: Renewed Calls for In-Person Testing," *Experience*, Senior Lawyers Division, American Bar Association, Vol. 18, No. 2, Winter, 2008, p. 13.

Institute for Highway Safety, there is a sharp increase in accidents for those drivers who are 80 and older.

Because the subject of whether or not an aging loved one should be driving is often so emotionally charged, people avoid talking about it. They don't want to upset their loved one. They fear that their loved one will get depressed, angry, upset with them, or refuse to talk to them. Their fears are well founded. Elders probably will get depressed, angry, upset or refuse to discuss the subject. However, the responsible adult child must step up and deal with this matter when the elder can't or won't.

If you just avoid it, every person walking on the street, and every driver on the road, is put at risk. If reluctance and discomfort are the worst things you could feel in discussing your elder's dangerous driving, please consider the worst thing the victim or victim's family could feel: grief that their own family member died or was hurt because someone failed to take the car keys away from the elder who should not be driving.

Whose Responsibility Is It? (Why Do *I* Have to Do It?)

Often, the aging person does not want to face the subject of impaired driving. It is the responsibility of the care giving family or the adult children of an elder who is clearly impaired, to look at the situation and take preventive action when the time comes. Leaving it entirely up to the elder to decide when to give up the car keys is not a safe choice. Too few elders will be that honest with themselves about their impaired driving. Worse yet, they may not actually realize how unsafe they have become behind the wheel and will be shocked or surprised to hear it.

Confusion, memory difficulty and thinking difficulty can happen to anyone. Sadly, elders who suffer from these problems can be so affected by them; they are no longer capable of clear judgment about their ability to drive safely. They may tell you their driving is just fine. You, the family member, have to take responsibility because the elder may simply be unable to do so.

See For Yourself -- Is Your Aging Loved One Safe On The Road?

You may never be able to find out if your aging loved one is safe on the road unless you get in the car with Mom, Dad or Granny, and observe their driving. If you have reason to think there may be a problem, do not take the elder's word for it that everything is fine. Denial is a big part of the problem. Lack of awareness can arise from a variety of sources also. Medications can cloud judgment or cause drowsiness, small strokes can impair reaction time and vision and memory loss may cause the elder to forget about the near accident of last week.

We encourage you to assess your aging loved one's situation to determine the risk level. There are various evaluation checklists available. One good example of a tool we suggest is the Texas Aging Network Senior Driving Assessment checklist, available online at TexasAgingNetwork.com and in the Appendix of this chapter. The checklist helps you, the concerned person, to systematically evaluate the driving performance of the elder. Other checklists are available from insurance companies and local programs designed to improve the driving skills of older drivers. Community-based safe driver programs for older drivers have tools to evaluate driving skills. The local department of vehicle licensing near your elder may have a course and evaluation available.

Ideally, one should ride along several times at different times of day to get a thorough idea of what the elder is actually doing behind the wheel. However, one can sometimes get enough "fear factor" in one trip to be convinced that the time has come for the elder to stop driving. If you think this ride-along and assessment sounds too formal and structured, just think about how formal and structured it might feel to be interviewed by the police after your elder crashes into something, hurts someone or worse. Possibly, with that picture in mind, you might feel motivated to overcome your own reluctance to tackle this difficult but necessary chore.

If your loved one does just fine when you ride along in the car at different times of the day and night, you do not need to take further steps at this time. However, a repeat of the ride-along should be done every few months. The fact is we all decline in one way or another with age, and the physical and mental faculties we need to be good drivers may also decline. If your aging loved one is not driving well on the ride-along, do not wait to bring up the subject. You could simply say, "Dad, I'm a little worried about you after driving with you. I think it's time to get a checkup from the doctor to see if everything is okay."

Getting a physical checkup is crucial to determining an elder's ability to drive safely. The medical doctor may see and know things about your loved one's condition that you never knew. The physician can be a very great help to you in broaching the subject of whether the elder should stop driving. You will need to accompany your loved one to the doctor or get his or her permission to talk with the doctor.

If you meet resistance from your loved one, you can and should write the doctor a short, respectfully worded letter, detailing your observations from driving with your loved one, voicing your safety concern about your elder's driving, and asking the physician for help. Enlist the help of other family members or friends, if possible, and add their names to the letter to the physician. You may think it's the elder's problem, and if he wants to take chances with his own safety, it's up to him. It isn't. Every day that passes with a dangerous driver on the road is a day of risk for everyone else.

If you have your doubts about your aging loved one's driving and he or she is willing to let an objective person evaluate his or her driving, there are professionals who can do this. Occupational therapy driving specialists can provide a thorough evaluation of driving skills and abilities, and do training as appropriate, to keep an older driver safe. These individuals are skilled in counseling and in educating elders about alternatives to driving, should it be found that your aging loved one is just not trainable any further. A statewide list of occupational therapists available to evaluate and train older drivers is located online at www1.aota.org/driver_search/index.aspx.

Further, new measurement tools for evaluating visual driving acuity are available online. Objective measurements and evaluations can be helpful if your elder is suspicious of your motives and doesn't trust your assessment of his or her driving capabilities from having you ride along.

Limited Driving May Be The First Step

There may be stages of declining driving ability in which the older driver is still safe with certain restrictions. For example, since vision usually decreases with age, particularly night vision, an elder may be willing to avoid driving at night. Additionally, slowing reaction time to driving situations also occurs with aging and your elder may agree to avoid freeway driving, driving in heavy traffic or driving to unfamiliar places. You have a better chance with self-imposed restrictions on driving, with the elder's agreement, than if you attempt to dictate them to the elder. These restrictions may enable the elder to keep the car keys longer. However, the burden may fall on the family members to increase the frequency of elder driving observation, as it is clear that a process is underway once any restriction is in place.

It is difficult to know how fast the process of decline will go, so it is up to loved ones to keep watch and protect the elder. One can only do this by increasing the amount of knowledge you have about the elder's driving by seeing it directly or getting a formal assessment. If you live at a distance from your aging loved one, you may need to make more visits. If that is not possible, you may need to enlist the help of a friend, neighbor or other contact who lives nearby your loved one to do the observing for you. Monitoring an elder's ability to drive on an ongoing basis is a safety issue for the elder as well as everyone else.

It can be very helpful to look for a way to make agreements with the elder about limiting his or her driving. If a change in physical status has occurred, such as a fall, a stroke, an illness, broken bone, or anything that changes mental alertness, it is a good time to bring up the subject of driving.

Medications and combinations of medications can have side effects, which are clear impediments to driving. The starting of a new medication may give you the opening you need to bring up the subject of limiting driving. A medication, of itself, may be the thing that causes a safety problem with driving. The elder's physician can help you find out about side effects of any new prescription, or effect of drug combinations your elder must take. You will need to ask. Many medical conditions can affect the ability to drive safely.

For many people, there is no single incident that paves the way to this subject. Rather, there is a gradual decline in the elder's alertness, memory, physical stamina, strength, ability to concentrate, reaction time, or any other ability necessary for safe driving. Over time, we start to notice these gradual changes. There may be no single event that makes it suddenly clear that there is a problem with driving.

If your aging loved one is willing to make agreements to limit driving, it is a fine first step. Asking for an agreement to limit driving allows a reasonable elder to choose to go along, and maintain a sense of control. Some lawyers advocate for getting the elder to appoint someone in the family or a trusted younger person to be the "agent" who will decide for the elder when it is time to give up the keys. It is much like appointing a power of attorney for making healthcare decisions. The agent may have only symbolic authority, but the process of writing out a document appointing the "agent," may do much to ease the decision making process when the time comes for an aging loved one to stop driving.

How Do I Bring Up The Subject?

For the adult children or other unimpaired family members, the aging person is not likely to invite you to start the conversation about driving. Don't expect to hear, "Hey kids, I think I'm a lousy driver. How 'bout taking the keys?" If you wait for Dad to initiate this, you will likely wait forever. If you know there is a problem with his driving, plan out what to do. Pick a time. After a birthday, new medication, trip to the hospital or other major event that reminds us of our mortality, it may be a good time to discuss the subject. People can be more amenable at such times to facing what no one likes to face, which is that we may be losing some of our abilities.

If you know it is time to address the problem driver, and a family gathering or holiday get together is planned, ask the family to set aside an extra day or time after the gathering to discuss matters. If you anticipate that your elder may be difficult, strategize with other family members about the best approach. Some conversations may start with such statements as, "Mom, now that you've had a stroke, we're not sure you can manage the car as well as before. I'd like to go with you for a ride to see if we need to make any adjustments with your driving."

Resistance might be addressed with such statements as "I really need you to do this for me, for my peace of mind." If you are able to enlist the help of the elder's physician, you can use factual information, such as, "Dr. Jones says the stroke affected your vision and we're worried about you not seeing someone coming at you in the car." The American Medical Association has adopted the explicit position that dealing with elders' driving issues should be a normal part of the basic physical and mental exam the doctor does for the patient. Your loved one's doctor may already have questioned her about her driving.

If you raise the subject with the doctor, the physician can provide a source of support, and an authoritative voice on the matter. If you notice dents in the car, paint scraped off or other evidence of "minor" collisions, you might approach the subject with something like this: "Grandma, we noticed the fender on your car was smashed and it hasn't been fixed. We'd like to help you. Was there an accident? Can we talk about it?" That may be a way to open the conversation about driving with grandma in as non-threatening a way as possible

As with any difficult subject, it will be necessary to bring the subject up respectfully, asking the elder's permission to talk about his or her driving. If the elder refuses to discuss it, you may try again later, within a short time frame. If that is not possible because you or others you want with you are not available later, you might insist gently, "We have to do this now, as I have to leave tomorrow." If you keep your tone even, your manner kind and your demeanor reassuring and loving, your chances are better than if you act otherwise.

Most people are frightened at the prospect of being questioned about their driving. Imagine how it would be for you, if you drive. One thing to avoid is telling the elder how it is going to be, without discussing it. Being bossy, forceful, demanding or accusatory can be very destructive and should be avoided.

It is no one's fault that we age. It is a fact of life that must be coped with, and your elder needs to cope. Allow for that to be. Anticipate that it may be upsetting to focus on it. Take your time. Be patient if you hear resistance. If it really is time to take the keys away, and the doctor is in agreement, be sure to mention that. Many elders look up to and go along with the doctor's word, even more than family's word. It is best to arrange for the doctor to tell his or her patient that driving is no longer safe. If that cannot be done, you may have to do it yourself.

What Can I Do With An Elder Who Has Dementia And Wants To Drive?

A diagnosis of dementia does not, by itself, mean that you know whether someone is capable of driving or not. At the beginning of the disease process of Alzheimer's, for example, driving may still be safe and the person may seem pretty normal. In the middle stage of Alzheimer's disease, driving becomes problematic.[2]

Though the middle stage may extend for three to five years, it is difficult to determine how far into the "middle stage" an elder has progressed. Therefore, it may be very difficult to predict when driving will become dangerous. It is imperative for anyone who has a loved one with a diagnosis of Alzheimer's disease, or other dementia, to closely watch your aging loved one for the first signs of unsafe driving.

You cannot leave it up to the elder to tell you when driving is becoming difficult. He or she may not have the perceptual ability to know this, as dementia is a progressive disease that damages the ability to remember as clearly as one could before having the disease. The first stage of Alzheimer's disease may also last for three to five years.

With that understanding, you have to be on the alert that by the time your aging loved one has had "early Alzheimer's" or "early dementia" for two years, it is definitely time to look very carefully at the risks of allowing him or her to continue driving. Very close monitoring by you is going to be necessary for safety. If you are in doubt, it is clearly safer to take the car keys away or get the elder's agreement to give them up if possible.

---

[2] P. Callone, C. Kudlacek, B. Basiloff, J. Manternach, R. Brumback, *A Caregiver's Guide to Alzheimer's Disease*, Demos Medical Publishing, 2006, p. 14.

There is a fuzzy line between "early dementia" and "middle stage" dementia or Alzheimer's, which creates problems for you, the family member or concerned person. No one can be sure how long the transition from one stage to another takes and we know from research that driving is definitely going to get dangerous at some point in the middle stage.[3]

Therefore, the family member or concerned person must be proactive and look for the trouble you know is coming. It is the only way to protect your elder unless he or she volunteers to give up driving under his or her own will. Above all, we caution against "waiting until there is an accident." It is not fair to other drivers and pedestrians to ignore the possible safety risks from an elder's dangerous dementia.

There is no doubt that people are living longer and the risk of all dementias rises with age. The National Institutes of Health estimates that one in seven people age 71 and older suffer from dementia.[4] Alzheimer's is the most prevalent kind of dementia and those 80 and older are much more likely to have dementia than those who are 70. Additionally, those in this age group have a sharp increase in accidents. If your elder is 80 or older, do not expect him or her to be an exception. The risk is there.

---

[3] Ibid., p. 14.

[4] Derocher, Robert J., "Licensing Older Drivers: Renewed Calls for In-Person Testing," *Experience*, Senior Lawyers Division, American Bar Association, Vol. 18, No. 2, Winter, 2008, p. 14.

What Can I Do To Make It Easier For My Loved One To Give Up Driving?

Although giving up driving is not easy, you can help. Start by communicating your respect for the difficulty loss of driving ability will mean to your elder. Acknowledge that the feeling of loss of control of one's driving must be really awful for the person going through it. Imagine having a brain disease that you know is going to get worse. Imagine how, little by little, you are aware of forgetting things and losing track of your daily activities. Imagine how hard it would be for an independent person to have to depend on others for basic things. Try to be as empathetic as possible and invite your elder to talk about it if he or she wishes to do so. Listen with an open heart and a kind attitude.

An important part of having your aging loved one give up driving rights is making some concrete arrangements to transport him or her to necessary activities. If Mom likes to get her hair done, and can't drive there anymore, provide a way for her to get to her hairdresser. Do not deprive Dad of his card game or other activities he loves when he can no longer drive.

Alternative transportation in general can be hard to find. In some communities, it is expensive. Research transportation services for elders in your community. Some communities offer low cost vans that pick up seniors at their residences and take them to appointments. Senior centers (sometimes called community centers) or other social service organizations in your parents' area may help solve the problem of transportation. Those who have the means may hire a home care worker to drive the elder to activities and appointments. Churches, synagogues and other nonprofit organizations serving those in need may also have transportation services.

Public transportation can be an option if it is available near his or her home, and if your elder can use it safely. However, if an elder is losing track of where he or she is, using the bus may not be safe, as a person with dementia can easily get lost. It may be up to family to provide the necessary transportation. If you live in a rural area where public transportation is not available, then family, friends and local organizations must fill the need.

The Independent Transportation Network is an example of an organization formed to create community-based transportation services for seniors throughout the country. It was founded by Katherine Freund, whose then 3-year-old son was struck and injured by a disoriented 84-year-old driver who thought he had hit a dog. If your aging loved one is no longer able to drive and needs transportation, research available resources in your community.

The absence of available transportation resources can force a change in living situation of an elder. Isolated seniors who may have to stop driving and do not have transportation resources available near their homes may also find it difficult to get the necessities of life, such as groceries and doctor's appointments. This scenario may bring the elder's living situation to a crisis point. If your elder is in a location where no transportation is offered and you live far away, think this through before you bring up the subject of driving.

Sometimes, the elder needs a little help with daily activities anyway, and would consider an assisted living situation or a household helper. Most assisted living facilities provide transportation for their residents, to doctors and to other social activities. If your aging loved one is at all ready to move to a supervised living setting, the issue of driving may be much easier to manage. A move could be the time to bring up giving up driving along with allowing the facility to provide transportation. For low-income seniors who have no community transportation options, family and friends may be the only alternatives.

What Can I Do If My Elder Absolutely Refuses To Give Up The Car Keys?

It is not unusual for an elder driver to refuse to give up the car keys, even if you, and everyone around you, believe it is the right thing to do. This is about the fear of losing control. As we age, we gradually lose control of some things we were always able to do before. Loss of control is a fear-provoking thing and many people will fight to keep what they perceive as control.

Refusing help at home is an example. An elder may equate having a helper with dependency, and loss of control, and refuse to allow even a helper for a few hours a week. Control is even more of an issue with driving, as not being able to drive truly is loss of control of one's independent travel. So, what can you do with this?

We advocate a five-level approach with taking legal action as an absolute last resort, when every other non-legal means has failed.

Level 1: One-on-one meeting

One can approach the subject of problematic driving in a tactful way, alone, at a quiet time, and when the elder seems to be in a good frame of mind. If tactful communication is not your strong suit, recruit someone else who has this skill. Another family member, friend or clergy may be willing to talk about this with your elder. Start with someone familiar, and someone who can remain calm. If you have siblings, choose the one most capable of having a difficult conversation or the person who feels closest to the elder.

If you are an only child or the only best friend of an aging loved one, it is up to you. Be straight with your loved one. "Mom, I'm very concerned about your safety. I would like to talk about it. It's about driving. Is it okay to talk about this now?" If you meet resistance, try again at another time. Keep trying and keep bringing it up. If your elder has a trusted lawyer, especially one who has prepared the trust or will, it may be useful to contact the lawyer. Let the lawyer know of your concerns and ask for a meeting between Mom or Dad and the lawyer.

However, remember that the attorney always represents his or her client, and that is not you. The lawyer will share your legitimate concerns about the elder's driving and may be a good source for the one-on-one meeting with your elder, especially if your loved one resists your advice. If this approach is not feasible or you are getting nowhere after several tries, consider moving to Level Two.

Level 2: Two-on-one meeting

If using a one-on-one approach with you or a trusted other does not work, and your aging loved one refuses to discuss his driving, it is time to go to the next level. Using two family members or friend/family members to bring up the subject together may get the much-needed results.

Any combination of adult child/lawyer, family member/clergy or other duo may be successful. This can be tricky, as the aging person may feel "ganged up on" if the twosome is forceful, pushy or fails to be respectful of the elder's resistance. It is always best to use the most liked, most favored or most trusted persons available for this task. The elder may be willing to listen to two others, whom he or she likes, respects and gets along with, to break the news that his or her driving has become a safety concern. If the twosome who approach the elder are both kindly in their approach, it has a better chance of success. Try more than once, if necessary. If that is also unsuccessful, it is time to try Level Three.

Level 3: Discussion with professional help

There are some people in the world who are just plain difficult, and if your elder is one of them, you may benefit from professional help with the issue of driving. Trained and skilled professionals, such as mediators, can do much to assist families who have communication difficulties get past this conflict-filled kind of conversation. It takes training to manage conflict among individuals who take opposing positions and then get "stuck."

Mediators are trained professionals who learn techniques to manage disputes. Most have a "peacemaking" personality, are good listeners, give everyone a chance to speak, keep order in the discussion, and guide people toward whatever solution they want to reach. Professional mediators are generally paid by the hour. Some work in low-cost community mediation centers, sometimes through the local county or city government, while others are privately retained through their own mediation businesses. Most courts have professionally trained mediators among members of the bar in your local county, as the courts use mediation often to resolve cases filed in courts.

To find a mediator in your area, check your local listings for your city or county, research mediators on the internet or contact the court administrator in your area and ask if a list of mediators is available. Some social workers work as mediators, though there is a distinct difference between social work and mediation, just as there is between therapy and mediation. Social workers who do conflict resolution in social service agencies would be suitable to assist with this kind of problem.[5]

We recommend use of a mediator or other trained, neutral person in situations where other attempts to work things out around

---

[5] Bertschler, Patricia and Laurette Cocklin, *Truce! Using Elder Mediation to Resolve Conflict Among Families, Seniors, and Organizations*, NCS Publishing, Independence, OH, 2004, pp. 35-38.

a dangerous driver have failed. Bringing in a professional can make a great difference, particularly in that it will permit the aging person a forum in which to be heard and respected. Often, after all involved have had a chance to speak about their perceptions of the problem in front of a neutral person, it is far easier to come to an agreement about what to do.

Level 4: Intervention

Failing other approaches, including mediation, consider the idea of a family "intervention." Intervention can mean many things, but in this context, it refers to a number of persons approaching an individual who has a problem. It is sometimes used with individuals who have a problem with drugs or alcohol, and are in denial about the problem.

As we suggest it here, intervention is a technique in which a group of loved ones including family, friends, and a leader (sometimes a professional such as an attorney, social worker, counselor, clergyperson or healthcare professional), meets with the elder to discuss the subject of driving and to end the danger.

An intervention may raise concern with families, or friends who are asked to participate. Some may feel that it is rude or intrusive. An intervention to address a dangerous driver's risk can be a lifesaving event. It is a profound act of caring.[6] An intervention requires an experienced person to lead the team and confront the

---

[6] Johnson, Vernon E., *Intervention: How to Help Someone who Doesn't Want Help*, Johnson Institute Books, Minneapolis, MN, 1986, p. 65.

driving issue with the reluctant or resisting elder. It differs from mediation in that mediation's purpose is to resolve conflict.

The purpose of an intervention is to stop to the danger presented by an elder's driving, reducing risk of injury or death to them or the public. It also differs from the kind of intervention used with those abusing a substance such as alcohol. Treatment is not the goal. The elder's problems of aging which cause him or her to be dangerous behind the wheel may not be amenable to treatment. Rather, the goal is to end the driving altogether.

The social worker or leader of the intervention is not neutral. His or her role is to help the chosen team of family and friends approach the elder about unsafe driving in a way that is non-destructive. An intervention can be overwhelming to anyone who is easily threatened and the technique should be used very carefully, again, with respect for the elder's point of view. The process must include an opportunity for the senior to speak about his or her point of view on the subject without interruption.

Then, others in a position to observe the elder's driving ability can bring up their various points of view and suggestions. Remaining factual ("There was a near collision last week when you were driving" or "Your eye doctor says it isn't safe to drive now") will be much more useful than being judgmental or saying anything the elder might think is insulting or demeaning, such as, "You're a bad driver" or "Are you trying to kill someone?"

The goal of this kind of intervention is to persuade the aging person to give up the car keys voluntarily. The use of a team of loved ones and/or trusted professionals and respectable others, who are all in agreement that it must be done, can help the elder to make the decision with a measure of dignity. A statement such as "All of us are worried about your driving since that ticket" or other consensus in the group can encourage a successful outcome. Reassurance to the elder that other means of transportation will be provided is essential. Remaining positive and loving throughout may lessen the blow to the elder, who may not have been aware of the concerns of family members and friends.

Everyone who participates in an intervention should be in agreement that the elder needs to give up driving. Do not invite anyone who may have a conflicted opinion, or who might believe the elder's driving ability is fine. This applies especially to any family or friends who are not in a position to know, as they have not been driving with the elder.

A united front is a critical part of this technique. All persons who participate should speak, in turn, to the elder about their fears and concerns about the elder's driving and say directly that they believe the elder must stop driving for his or her own safety, as well as the safety of others. The leader of the intervention can ask the elder to hand over the car keys to him or her. It is a form of "peer pressure," in that everyone is in agreement that the elder is in danger if he/she continues to drive. It is a direct request to give up driving voluntarily. Failing that, it is an agreement to get the keys away, keeping the elder fully informed of why, even though he or she may be in complete denial.

The risks of using a group intervention to approach the elder are that the elder may become very frightened, embarrassed or resistant out of fear. He or she could lash out and become enraged. She could refuse to speak to anyone. He could walk away and leave everyone sitting there. However, the risks may be worth the effort if you succeed. Having someone agree to give up driving rights is certainly better than forcing the decision on him. Preserving the elder's dignity is paramount. Stopping the dangerous behavior must occur if the intervention is to be successful.

Preparation for an intervention is critical. The leader must communicate with everyone and form a plan. The elder should be informed that this planning is taking place. Transparency of the planning process can reduce the suspiciousness and anger on the part of the elder.

We do not advocate hiding or stealing the car keys, using tricks, disabling the car without telling the elder, or other secretive methods to stop an elder from driving. All of these actions are less than honest and are more likely to cause the elder to become suspicious, enraged or even punitive in retaliation for being tricked. It is only fair to discuss the possible plans with the elder, rather than have him or her go to get in the car and discover that it will not start because someone has disabled it.

One of our elderly clients whose family tried the above sneaky methods to get the elder to stop driving got so angry, he had another set of keys made and threatened to disinherit his daughter and son for taking his keys. They did not stop him. Damage to the family relationships from the dishonesty of stealing the keys was devastating. Other approaches could have been tried, but other options were not attempted. Eventually, the department of motor vehicles did not renew his license

In another instance, an elder had had several minor "fender bender" accidents. Finally, she had a more serious collision and totaled her car turning in front of another driver. Fortunately, no one was injured. After the last accident, the family approached her to explain why they were not going to replace the car, a task she could not have done without their help.

It would have been much safer for this family to try one of the four steps recommended above *before* the final accident happened. They waited, because she kept saying, "I'm fine to drive." None of the adult children wanted to get in a fight with their mother about stopping her from driving. After the first or second minor accident, it was time to ask her to voluntarily give up her car keys. It was sheer luck that when she totaled the car, she did not hurt or kill anyone else. Do not let this be your elder. The gamble with safety is too great.

Level 5: Using the law as a last resort

Finally, there are possible legal means that can be used as a last resort, only if your aging loved one is truly a danger on the road in a specific and provable way. First, you could try the approach of requesting a letter from your elder's medical doctor to be sent to the local department of motor vehicles, describing that the elder is no longer able to drive safely. You could ask your aging loved one's doctor to recommend an occupational therapist's evaluation of the elder's driving skills.

Your state's laws are not universal when it comes to aging drivers, so the result of communicating with your motor vehicle licensing department may vary from state to state. The local department of motor vehicles can issue a letter to a licensed driver, asking him or her to turn in the license voluntarily.

Typically, the state does not have the authority to suspend or revoke a driver's license unless the driver has failed a written test, vision or driving test at license renewal time; or there has been an accident, traffic violation or event that generates a police report, highway patrol report or event that brings the aging driver before the court. In those instances, the traffic officer may recommend that the license of the offending driver be taken away. The court can decide to suspend or revoke a license. However, it will not necessarily do so based on the request of someone other than law enforcement.

A physician's letter to the state licensing department for motor vehicles can help. The licensing agency likely has the authority to revoke a license based on a medical doctor's recommendation. This occurs with individuals who have seizure disorders, such as epilepsy, which can make a driver unsafe. The same concept can apply to an impaired older driver.

Sometimes, it literally takes an accident for a police officer to see the elder, talk with him or her, and find evidence of confusion or disorientation to the degree that the officer believes the person who caused the accident should not be driving. Driving is a right, as it is considered part of our freedom under the Constitution. Therefore, states are obligated to see proof that this right should be taken away in the interest of public safety. Even if there is an accident or incident and the department of motor vehicles suspends or revokes a driver's license, the driver normally has a right to appeal this decision and request a hearing. In states where it works this way, the driver has the right to present evidence of his or her ability to drive, which could result in the suspension being lifted or changed.

Some elders even hire attorneys to represent them at such hearings and are successful in getting their driver's licenses restored. For others, however, the revocation of a license can become permanent as a result of a hearing, if the hearing officer finds insufficient evidence that the driver can drive safely. If and when a dangerous incident has come up, and the family is concerned, the elder's doctor can be contacted. One could ask the doctor to order an occupational therapy driving assessment.

With the results of the assessment showing that the elder is not a safe driver, the doctor is obligated to cooperate with efforts to end the elder's driving privileges. A letter to the department of motor vehicles from the physician, with the occupational therapist's driving assessment attached, may be enough to get the elder's license revoked.

What To Do When Your Elder Is A Danger To Herself Or Others

Suppose your elder is a dangerous driver, has nearly hit several cars, scares the life out of you when you are in the car with her, and you know she should not be driving. She refuses a driving assessment by an occupational therapist or anyone else, and her driver's license is good for two more years. You have tried to arrange a meeting, but she won't discuss it, and the two-person approach also failed. You don't know her doctor's name because she won't tell you.

Everyone in the family, and several neighbors and friends, tried the "intervention" approach, but she started screaming at everyone to get out of her house when the subject of driving came up. You are truly afraid, as is everyone in the family that she is going to kill someone, or herself. She got lost in the grocery store last week, has fallen several times, left the stove burner on several times last month, without remembering, and almost started a fire. However, she still refuses to agree to limited driving and won't turn over the car keys. Is there anything else you can do?

There is one last thing to do, and it is the drastic step of guardianship, also called conservatorship. More details of a guardianship/conservatorship can be found in the "How to Handle

Money for Aging Loved Ones" chapter. Briefly, getting a guardianship means going to court to get an order from a judge appointing someone to be a "guardian" or "conservator" of the person. That person then has authority to act for the person under guardianship. That authority includes legally stopping the elder from driving. In this example, the aging person does many dangerous things, and the issue is safety, to an extreme degree.

Whether handling money is also an issue or not is up to the lawyer preparing the matter for court to help you decide. It can be included in the guardianship proceeding as necessary. Aging persons who have trouble remembering to turn off the stove often have problems handling money, as well. The troubles they are having could be symptoms of dementia or other disease processes. These same disease processes can cause the driver to become unsafe behind the wheel.

The guardianship proceeding is not a simple matter. A lawyer is normally needed to help prove that an elder needs this serious protection, as a guardianship takes away major freedoms for the person upon whom it is imposed. The courts, through judges or "commissioners" who hear the evidence, are required to take steps to see that the rights of the individual are not taken away without very clear and weighty proof.

In other words, the evidence presented to demonstrate to the judge or commissioner that the elder should have a guardian must be very strong. The elder, for whom guardianship is proposed, has a right to present evidence that a guardianship is *not* needed.

Therefore, in order to prove that many basic freedoms, which can include driving, should be taken away, the person asking for the guardianship for an elder has to have a doctor to verify that the person is in serious danger without the guardianship.

In the earlier example of the elder with dementia (the elder who will not talk about her driving, has had near accidents, gets lost, keeps falling, leaves the stove on, etc.) testimony from witnesses would be needed to prove that these things occurred, and that she is considered to be a danger to herself and others.

If there is sufficient proof, the judge may decide to grant the guardianship, and will appoint a person, preferably a family member, to be the guardian of the person in question. The guardian then has the legal right to take the necessary precautions, including taking the car and keys away from the elder, to protect the elder and others from danger.

Getting a guardianship is best done by an attorney experienced in these matters. Elder law attorneys are the most likely to have the necessary experience to handle this kind of case. We urge anyone who is thinking about a guardianship to seek legal advice, and to consider the pros and cons very carefully before going forward. (See the "How to Find a Good Lawyer" chapter for more information.)

The risks of getting a guardianship are many. It costs money to hire an attorney to go to court. Even if the person seeking a guardianship is low income and qualifies for free legal services, there is a significant cost in terms of time and stress associated with the proceedings. It is possible that the elder could convince the court that his or her driving and other problems are not dangerous, and that a guardianship is not needed. Skilled use of evidence is how lawyers win cases, including guardianship cases.

However, the decision is up to the judge. The courts are required to protect the rights of elders and must look very carefully at the reasons for the request for a guardianship. Therefore, it is not automatically granted by the courts. In the earlier example of the difficult elder, she may hire an attorney of her own in an attempt to prevent the guardianship or conservatorship from being imposed. If the elder makes a good impression on the judge, speaks clearly, and appears to be of sound mind, the court may be unwilling to impose a guardianship. This can leave all parties involved angry, dissatisfied and distrustful of each other.

An additional risk of a guardianship proceeding is that the elder may become very angry that he or she is being "betrayed" by the person(s) seeking to place him or her under a guardianship. It can fracture family relationships, cause emotional trauma to all involved and leave a bitter, hostile family environment in its wake. However, this does not always happen. Sometimes, the elder needs to have a judge appoint a guardian so that he or she can finally give up the car keys, and give up the other things which make him a danger to himself. It can resolve the matter and provide a means to protect the elder in many other ways, as well. We call it a last resort, as *it should only be used in extreme situations, when there is no alternative.*

However, in the example described earlier, it is a reasonable choice of action. A car can certainly be a lethal weapon. A guardianship provides a legal way to stop a dangerous driver from injuring or killing anyone with a car. It should never be attempted unless it is absolutely necessary for safety of the elder, and safety of others.

An important other consideration about a guardianship/ conservatorship is the fact that the guardian or conservator may not be honest or may not have the elder's best interests at heart. The risk increases when there is no family member willing to take on the burdensome responsibility of being the guardian, and the court appoints a stranger to the elder.

Guardians have almost unlimited power over the person who becomes their "ward" or protected person. As with any situation in which there is almost unlimited power, the temptation for unlimited corruption exists. It is far better to use a family member if one is capable and willing, than to go outside the family. Therefore, weigh the possibilities carefully and use this legal means to protect the elder only when it is the only reasonable alternative to preventing the most serious kinds of harm. If it is the only alternative available, spend the money and go forward.

Here is a true story of a dangerous older driver. One wonders why the family, friends, clergy or doctor of 93-year-old Ralph Parker of St. Petersburg, Florida did not seek a guardianship over him prior to this incident in 2005. He struck and killed a pedestrian, and then drove three miles with the dead (victim's) body lodged in his windshield.

According to The American Bar Association publication, *Experience*, which reported this story in its Winter 2008 issue, Mr. Parker thought the body "had fallen from the sky." [7] Surely, someone must have known before this tragedy that Mr. Parker was a danger to himself and others. He should not have been driving, yet, he was. Perhaps he thought he was fine. Do not let this happen to you or your elder.

Summary

Driving is a right in our society, for those who can pass the driving tests and get a license. Giving up this right or having it taken away is a serious matter. Loss of control is very important to most of us. It is unfair to others to ignore a dangerous older driver, despite the reality that the elder may lose control of the right to drive. Caring family members must collect information, approach the subject respectfully, and in some cases, take steps to limit or end the dangerous driver's chances of injuring himself or someone else.

---

[7] Derocher, Robert J., "Licensing Older Drivers: Renewed Calls for In-Person Testing," *Experience*, Senior Lawyers Division, American Bar Association, Vol. 18, No. 2, Winter 2008, pp. 13-16.

Ten Tips for Handling a Dangerous Older Driver

---

1. Recognize that this is difficult subject matter, approach it carefully, and respect the elder's need for control.
2. Ride along with your elder to see firsthand if there is a problem with driving.
3. If you see a problem with your aging loved one's driving, and it is serious, do not avoid the subject because it is uncomfortable. Keep in mind the risks to those who could be injured by a dangerous driver.
4. Try discussing the matter at a good time, in a thoughtful way, and let the elder know that you are concerned if you see a problem with his/her driving.
5. If you suggest giving up or limiting driving, suggest alternative transportation.
6. If an informal discussion is not effective, plan a formal one with you and your loved one. Ask your elder's permission to have it.
7. If the one-on-one approach does not work, try two-on-one. Move to the next level of facilitated discussion (also called mediation), if you are not getting anywhere. If that fails, try the next level, which is a family and friends intervention, if appropriate.
8. Ask your elder's doctor to write a letter to your motor vehicle department describing that the elder is no longer capable of driving safely. Remember that this is only a request and may not result in formal action because the elder has a right to

drive until law enforcement, or the court, decide to revoke a driver's license.

9. Consider guardianship or conservatorship as an absolute last resort. The elder who needs this will have multiple problems that cause him or her to be a danger, and the court will need strong proof of it, before the court will take away one's freedom by a guardianship or conservatorship.
10. Keep in mind that elders may no longer have the ability to tell that they are impaired and their driving has become dangerous to their own safety and that of the public. Help your aging loved one when driving becomes unsafe.

A group of Sun City senior citizens was sitting around talking about their ailments:

"My arms are so weak I can barely hold a cup of coffee," said one.

"Yes, I know. My cataracts are so bad I can't even see my coffee," replied another.

"I can't turn my head because of the arthritis in my neck," said a third, to which several nodded in agreement.

My blood pressure pills make me dizzy," another went on.

"I guess that's the price we pay for getting old," winced an old man as he shook his head.

Then there was a short moment of silence.

"Well, it's not that bad," said one woman cheerfully. "Thank God, we can all still drive"!

Appendix

Texas Aging Network - Senior Driving Assessment Checklist

Rider/Assessor ____________________________

Date ____________ Time __________

If you are concerned about an older driver's safety on the road, the best way to evaluate his or her driving ability is to ride along. Use the checklist below to record your observations after (not during) your ride. If you can, ask several people to take rides at different times of the day.

√	Action	Comment
	Ran a red light	
	Ignored or misinterpreted traffic lights, stop signs, yield signs	
	Did not appear to notice other vehicles, pedestrians, bicycles or road hazards	
	Had a near miss	
	Had difficulty physically while driving (did not look over shoulder or to the rear when appropriate, or had trouble turning the wheel).	
	Did not look or yield when pulling out of parking space or driveway	
	Crossed into other lanes when driving straight	

	Drove too close to the car ahead	
	Did not stay in lane when turning	
	Drove aggressively	
	Drove too slowly	
	Stopped inappropriately	
	Did not signal correctly	
	Did not anticipate potential danger or changing traffic conditions (slowing down when brake lights appeared ahead)	
	Ran over a curb	
	Asked passengers whether the road was clear	
	Became frustrated or irritated	
	Appeared confused or frightened	
	Parked inappropriately	

If you checked any of the six items in the **"Gray Zone,"** your older driver should be prevented from driving, at least temporarily, while you further investigate.

1. Have your older driver's vision and hearing tested

2. Schedule a complete physical examination where the doctor will pay particular attention to physical reflexes and any medications, which might be contributing to confusion or drowsiness.

3. If you are certain that your driver is a danger behind the wheel and should not be driving, as a last resort, you can make a report to the Medical Advisory Board of the Texas Department of Public Safety. Anyone can make a report, including physicians, family, friends, and acquaintances. Your report must be in writing. In your report, you must identify the Texas driver with full name and date of birth or Texas driver license number.

These reports may be kept confidential, unless the subject requests the document through an open records request. All records are subject to becoming open records if the person requests an administrative hearing, which is unlikely, but not impossible.

Send your written concern to:
Texas Department of Public Safety
PO Box 4087
Austin, TX 78773-0320
Attention: Driver Improvement Bureau

For more information **on Senior Driving Safety,** visit theTexas Department of Public Safety website.

References

Bertschler, Patricia and Laurette Cocklin, 2004. *Truce! Using Elder Mediation to Resolve Conflict among Families, Seniors, and Organizations*. Ohio: NCS Publishing.

P. Callone, C. Kudlacek, B. Basiloff, 2003. *A Caregiver's Guide to Alzheimer's Disease*. New York: Demos Medical Publishing.

Derocher, Robert J. "Licensing Older Drivers: Renewed Calls for In-Person Testing." Experience, Senior Lawyers Division American Bar Association Vol. 18, No. 2 (Winter 2008): 13-16.

Johnson, Vernon E., 1986. *Intervention: How to Help Someone Who Doesn't Want Help*. Minneapolis, MN: Johnson Institute Books.

Texas Aging Network, PO Box 700291, Dallas, TX 75370 **http://www.texasagingnetwork.com**

Chapter Two
How to Choose a Home Care Worker

Introduction

When an aging parent or other loved one starts to lose the ability to do everyday things alone, such as bathing or cooking, the elder or her family may consider getting a helper. There may be resistance to the idea of help initially. For some elders, having to rely on a helper for anything is stressful and threatening. It can have a symbolic meaning, that "I'm going downhill" or "becoming a burden." Many elders resist "having a stranger in my house."

However, when the effects of aging prevent a loved one from managing his or her daily life alone, it is time to find out if help at home can solve the problem. The arena of home care workers is largely unregulated by government and by society in general. It is usually considered a private matter, which it is. The difficulty is that many people hire someone to work in the home on their own (without using an agency), and in doing so, they take more risks than they may realize.

This chapter is an effort to educate adult children of aging parents, or the parents themselves, of the danger in hiring home care workers, especially without the help of an agency. It is also a guide to assist you through the process, giving you information about what to expect and how to do the hiring in a legal way.

As technology has developed, we have the means to check out anyone we hire to do anything. Sometimes, it just doesn't occur to a person who wants to hire a home care worker that being too trusting can be a costly mistake. For elders who may be more trusting than their adult children, a smiling face, friendly manner, and pleasant conversation may be enough to cause them to trust a person who applies for a home care worker job. Many a con artist and thief have the ability to fool an elder with a pleasant demeanor.

I encourage every person who wishes to bring a worker into the home to get thorough information, to do a criminal background check, as well as a job history background check. Agencies should be doing this kind of screening. If you aren't sure what an agency is doing to check their workers' backgrounds, please ask a lot of detailed questions about it.

Your elder is at risk for financial and other abuse simply because of age, and particularly, because of dementia and other conditions which affect mental ability. Many home care workers are kind, dedicated folks who enjoy taking care of elders. They enable Mom or Dad to stay at home, where most elders prefer to be, and to manage their activities of daily living safely. However, not all are honest. A home setting is unsupervised and can be very tempting for a dishonest person to take advantage of the aging person receiving care. The message is simply: beware, and if home help is needed, get it the smart way.

How to Choose a Home Care Worker

If you have noticed that your aging loved one is not managing so well on his or her own, you are probably considering getting help at home. As people age, they begin demonstrate for us some of the signs of aging, which include loss of physical strength, memory difficulty, and the inability to keep track of things. The combination of these problems, which may or may not include disease processes such as dementia, arthritis, and other ailments, may result in a decline in independence.

It is certainly a common trait that the elder, him or herself, is not the first to recognize a decline in independence. It seems to be something we naturally resist. We do not want to admit that we cannot be completely on our own or that we are not as capable as we used to be. To do so, would be to recognize that we are getting closer to the ends of our lives, and this is not something our society accepts.

In a country in which youth is highly valued, and age may be disrespected by many, the aging process and the need for help at home often meet resistance. Resistance to recognizing the need for help often comes from the elder. Sometimes, the family members also resist recognizing an elder's decline. Facing it means facing that Mom or Dad is getting old, could be in failing health, and may die sooner rather than later. No one likes to deal with this, but the "head in the sand" approach can lead to disaster.

Perhaps on your last visit to your aging parents you discovered that the house, which was always neatly kept, has been neglected. The yard has not been tended to, nor the grass mowed. Mom's clothes are dirty, and she was always very fastidious. There is not much food in the house. Prescription medicine bottles are in disorder, and some are empty. You may have been worrying about this for some time, and you have finally come to the conclusion that is time to approach your aging loved ones with the subject of getting help.

Unfortunately, many people are in crisis when they finally start looking for a homecare worker. If you are a responsible relative, it is not smart to wait until your loved one falls at home, gets hospitalized, or you get a frantic call from a neighbor about your loved one. With some guidelines in mind, you can do the best job possible of finding a homecare worker and prevent the disasters that come from lack of planning.

Recommendations For Choosing A Home Care Worker To Assist Your Aging Loved One

The following are recommendations as to what you can do to be a good consumer.

1. Spend some time doing research about how to locate the best care giving resource. Failure to do adequate research and preparation can lead you to placing an incompetent worker in a loved one's home, financial or other elder abuse, or related criminal activity, and even physical assault. It may take you two

or three hours to look into agencies or other resources in your community or the community where your aging loved ones reside. However, it is time that must always be spent to best honor the needs of the person you care about. Check local listings if you wish to do the hiring on your own. Talk to at least a few agencies if you wish to go through an agency to hire a homecare worker.

The pros and cons of going to an agency versus hiring someone on your own are discussed below. Remember that your elder can rapidly decline at home if the care provided to him is inadequate. Injury or financial ruin can arise from the wrong caregiver.

2.Be involved. If you live out of the area where your loved one resides, hire a geriatric care manager to assist you. (See the *"How to Find and Use a Care Manager"* chapter for more information.) If you do not have the means to hire a geriatric care manager to assist you in locating the best agency for aging loved one, look for an agency which is very communicative and has a care management aspect.

Some agency managers have no contact with the family or client's family after the worker is placed. Other agencies have frequent contact with the client's family, the physician, social worker, and other involved persons in a "team approach." Ask about the agency's policy of being involved with the family of the elder after a worker is placed in the home.

3.Be sure to inquire about what kind of background and qualifications check and what training is done by the agency before workers are hired. Find out how much oversight and supervision the agency provides to its workers. Inquire about the frequency and method of communication with you, the person who is requesting placement of a worker in the home. Find out how long the agency has been in business, whether it is insured, and how many people are in charge of administration.

4.Be sure a thorough and professional needs assessment is done at the time a home worker is placed to assist your aging loved one. Many agencies use an assessment tool, such as a checklist or questionnaire. Take a look at it, ask to see the paperwork, find out who does the assessment and their qualifications and experience in doing so.

5.Involve the elder as much as possible in the entire process. If your aging loved one has limited mental capacity due to Alzheimer's disease, or other dementia or conditions, their participation may be limited. However, persons in the earlier stages of dementia are still capable of participating, voicing an opinion, and providing their input. Generally, it is a mistake to simply march in and tell your aging parent what is going to happen. No one wants to lose a feeling of control over one's life. This is a critical issue.

If your loved one's mental status will allow, ask them to express their wishes, preferences, likes, and dislikes. Insofar as it is safe to do so, ask your elder to choose the right agency and the right worker.

If your elder is resistant to the idea of placing someone in his or her home, be sure that you discuss it thoroughly and well in advance of bringing an agency representative or care manager into the home. Even if your loved one refuses to choose or give an opinion, make the effort to ask him or her to do so before choosing for the elder.

6.Do a thorough safety inspection of the elder's home before a worker is placed there. Everything from removing throw rugs to reconstructing bathrooms and building ramps should be considered, depending on what the elder needs. Be sure that home care is a safe and appropriate choice for the elder rather than placement in assisted living, board and care, or other facility.

If the home is unsafe, not suitable, and cannot be appropriately remodeled to accommodate the elder's changing needs, home care is not a wise choice. An elder may not be safe at home just because he or she says, "I'll never go to one of 'those places for old people.'" The deciding factor should be the elder's capability to remain there with help, while not endangering the elder.

7.Compare home care as a choice with other choices available to you and your elder. Perhaps the social isolation of remaining at home is not the best choice. On the other hand, if your aging loved one has friends and other social connections, and is able to get out to activities; home care for a time may be a perfectly reasonable option. If your elder is deprived of company, a communal living situation such as assisted living may be better and safer. Home care for an elder who is very isolated may limit social stimulation too much to be healthy for the elder.

If I Go With An Agency, What Should I Look For?

An agency should be well-established, and should be able to provide you with references. It should have a written contract or price list spelling out the charges involved and the kinds of services it can provide. If you are not sure about signing a contract, you may have it reviewed by a lawyer. However, most of the things home care agencies provide are non-medical, common sense services. It is not necessary to seek legal advice to review a service contract of this kind, unless there is any part of it about which you are confused or if the agency is unable to answer your questions. If you have any doubt, seek legal advice.

The agency should provide a thorough assessment of your elder's needs at the outset. This should include a general assessment of the elder's physical, emotional, and psychosocial needs, as well as a review of the physical environment. Safety should also be one of the major concerns the agency has as a priority.

Following an assessment, the agency should give the consumer suggestions as to what the elder's needs are as the agency has assessed them. You should be able to expect input from an agency, as their representative may be able to see things you have missed or that the elder has not told you about.

The agency should communicate with the elder's adult children or other relatives about the frequency and amount of home care they believe the elder needs. Many agency representatives have years of experience doing such assessments and they can be quite helpful to you, the consumer, in making suggestions. Family members may not have a clear understanding of what the elder's needs really are. This comes from the fact that the elder may not live with their adult children, that the elder may not clearly describe the problems he or she is having, and the fact that the elder's needs are probably changing as time goes by.

According to Erin Winter, co-owner of Hired Hands Homecare Inc. (www.HiredHandsHomecare.com) in Novato, California, "about 75% of the elders we serve don't think they need help when it is obvious to those around them that they do." Working through the elder's resistance is the first step. One must respect the elder, yet gently push ahead, presenting the idea of help for the sake of the peace of mind of the adult child. Ms. Winter indicates that this is an approach that works. The elder may agree to "try it." The adult child or other relative may be able to persuade the elder to accept some help by describing that they need to have more peace of mind while they are at work or with their own families, or because they live out of the area.

Once help is in place, it is rare for the elder to reject the person who regularly comes to offer assistance. If the worker shows up each time with a kindly and respectful attitude and asks the elder what he or she would like, it can induce the elder to stick with having this help. Again, helping the elder maintain a sense of control is very important.

Elders will often tell us "I've been doing fine all by myself and I don't need any help." No one seems to be quite ready to believe that he or she needs assistance with ordinary things. However, acknowledging and honoring the elder's belief in his or her own independence, while reminding him that the adult relative or child needs reassurance that the elder is safe, can be a good approach.

What Are The Advantages And Disadvantages Of Hiring A Home Worker On Your Own?

Advantages

It is possible to hire a qualified and good home worker on your own without going through an agency. The main advantage is that you will save money. The home care business is a profit-making business, and the people who are sending workers into individual homes need to make a profit in order to stay viable. They will charge more, in most cases, than you will pay if you do not use an agency. *We recommend that you always use an agency to place a worker in your home*. We believe that the risks are not worth the relatively small cost difference of going through a reputable agency to get a competent worker to help your elder at home.

Disadvantages

There are many disadvantages to hiring someone on your own. They include these things:

1. Lack of expertise in getting a thorough background check of a worker. You may not have the resources or knowledge to do a thorough screening and criminal background check. Background-checking services are available and agencies may contract for these at a reduced rate. An individual will have to spend money out of pocket, find a good background checking service, and get the information coming from the background check before hiring a helper. Without an agency, you have to do all the screening yourself. You must call references, search public records, conduct more than one interview, and the process can be daunting.

2. Lack of experience in screening potential workers. You may not have experience in screening and hiring people to do work in the home. This can be a disadvantage. People who are looking for this kind of work as a way of finding an opportunity to commit elder financial abuse may present very well, and may be congenial, experienced and warm. It is much easier to be fooled by this if you are hiring someone for the first time than if you hire people as a part of your daily business. Experienced agency employers may have developed a "nose" for the unsuitable worker. It could be that

you, as an individual, trying to hire on your own, lack the sophistication and skill to hire smart.

3. The risk of theft. Theft can be committed by any worker in the home. The worker is left alone with the elder for a couple of hours each day to many hours each day. Opportunities to take advantage of the situation and steal, commit identity theft, or even abuse the elder are there. Home workers are unsupervised when there is no agency involved. Individual workers not screened by agencies may be uninsured and unbonded, so you have no way to recover from a theft of money or property by an independent worker. An agency is likely to carry insurance and be bonded to protect you against loss from theft.

4. The need to report the worker's earnings and to withhold taxes for any employee you hire. According to the Internal Revenue Service, anyone who employs a private person on a regular basis at home, has an employee, rather than an independent contractor. Accordingly, you, the employer, must withhold taxes according to the law, pay payroll tax, and report the earnings of your worker.

5. Worker's compensation insurance. If you hire a home worker, set the home worker's hours and require that they work on specific days, technically, the home worker is your employee. The rules vary from state to state with regard to what worker's compensation insurance you must purchase, but in some states it is necessary for any employee to have

worker's compensation insurance as a matter of law. The workers compensation insurance premium may be something you did not plan on paying. It may be a requirement of your state's law that you have it, because workers can be injured on the job with lifting, carrying, and doing some of the many other things which elders require. Back injuries among caregivers are fairly common.

You could be liable for all medical costs for such an injury if your homecare worker, hired independently, does not have insurance to cover medical expenses in the event of injury on the job.

6. Unemployment insurance. Unemployment insurance may also be a state requirement for any employee, even a part-time employee. Check with your local and state laws to determine if you must purchase unemployment insurance for any worker, even a part-time worker who is employed in the home. If the worker gets fired, the worker can then collect unemployment insurance until he/she has found a replacement job.

7. The need to personally check the worker's driving record. It will be necessary for you to check the driving record of any person whom you wish to either drive your elder's vehicle or who will transport your elder in their own vehicle. You will need to determine whether the worker's license is valid in your state. Most states require some form of liability insurance on the automobile that will be driven. It

will be necessary for you to determine that the liability insurance policy covering either or both vehicles you expect the worker to drive is current and adequate for the vehicle and for any person injured while driving it.
Again, this can take time. An agency which screens its workers (as a qualified agency should do), will have workers ready to go when you call. The check for proper driver's license and insurance will already be done.

8. Independent workers may lack stability. If you are hiring on your own, it is necessary to contemplate the possibility that the worker will suddenly quit and leave your elder without help. Workers who come from other countries may have to leave if a family member in their country of origin becomes ill or dies. The worker may get sick and be unable to work. Since one cannot necessarily anticipate such a situation in advance, you may hear, without any notice that your worker has suddenly departed for another location and you are left with any sense of when that person will return. You, as a responsible relative, can suddenly get stuck caring for your elder who has no help at home. This can interfere with your job, family, and your own responsibilities.

It is extremely difficult to find help on your own to replace a worker who departs suddenly, if your elder needs help each day. The process of background checking, checking references, and the like cannot be done instantly. An agency will work to provide you with another worker as fast as they possibly can, in order to keep you as a customer.

9. Independent workers may be unreliable in assisting with medications. Elders often have trouble keeping track of medications, keeping their prescriptions filled, and remembering when to take the medications which are prescribed for them. If an agency is involved, the agency representative or care manager can set up a system to ensure that the elder takes medicines at the proper time and in the proper amount. The agency representative can be sure that there are proper refills when the elder has run out of medication. In addition, a home worker may or may not, without supervision, be able to tell you when side effects from a medication occur, or when a medication seems to be producing a bad result.

Although many agencies do not provide licensed or highly skilled workers with any medical training, managers of the agencies who employ the caregivers can at least tell you the obvious problems that seem to be connected to the starting of a new medication, particularly if you ask for this information. If you live nearby your aging loved one and can check in on him or her each day, you can monitor the medications yourself.

If you live at some distance, and cannot be there on a daily basis, it is much more difficult to ensure that the home worker that you hired on your own will report things to you as you wish them to be reported. An agency may be more likely to provide the service of setting up a workable plan for medication assistance than an untried worker could do.

What Can I Expect From An Agency?

An agency may cost you more than trying to hire on your own, but the extra money you will need to pay an agency to find you a qualified worker is well worth it. Quality agencies are in the business of providing competent home workers. Most of the time, the home worker provides companionship services such as transporting the client to appointments, assistance with shopping and errands, reading and assistance with correspondence, purchasing of groceries, cooking and providing meals, and doing light housekeeping. The companionship services may also include reminding the elder to take medications at specific times throughout the day. For an elder with memory problems, you should not chance hiring an incompetent worker.

In addition, an agency will provide hands on care giving services such as bathing, dressing, washing hair, grooming nails, transferring from bed to chair, chair to bath, and back to bed, help with walking, and help with exercise programs. It is not what Medicare refers to as "skilled nursing." Care giving services are not provided by people who are licensed nurses or have nursing training in a formal program. It is considered unskilled or "custodial" services. Medicare does not pay for custodial services. If your elder needs a variety of custodial services, an agency will know the person best suited to meet your elder's needs.

Home care agencies will also often provide overnight shifts if elders cannot be alone at night. Most agencies will also supply workers providing the elder with care 24 hours a day. If you are attempting to hire on your own, it may be very difficult to safely find workers to cover 24-hour care. If your worker suddenly quits, an agency will supply an interim worker until a permanent replacement is found. Many agencies guarantee this service.

What you cannot expect from any agency is perfection. Workers who are carefully screened do not always meet their employer's expectations, as in any employment situation. You are responsible to make sure that your elder is safe, well cared for, and that the agency is doing its job. If you are not satisfied with what the agency has provided, it is appropriate to express your dissatisfaction, and ask for another worker. It is necessary to involve your aging loved one in the process when possible, as change can be much harder for elders than for more adaptable, younger people. Never change workers without asking your elder about it, making respectful suggestions, preparing your elder, and trying to get the elder to agree to the change.

Hired Hands Homecare Inc., Novato, California, (www.HiredHandsHomecare.com) has courteously provided us with a sample checklist of things to ask an agency if you are considering hiring a homecare worker. You can find it in the Appendix of this chapter. We recommend that you use this checklist, or one that suits your needs, before you decide which agency to hire.

Do All Agencies Employ Their Caregivers?

All agencies should thoroughly screen, background check, insure, and bond every worker they provide for you, but not all home care agencies are the employers of the workers they place with you. Agencies which serve as employers for their own workers assume responsibility for payroll, taxes, insurance, invoicing your aging parent or you, and receiving payment, including checks, credit cards, or long-term care insurance, which covers such services. Generally, assessment by an agency representative is provided without additional charge.

Non-employer agencies, which function as placement agencies only, do not typically provide supervision of their workers, though some "placement" agencies may offer limited supervision. Ongoing supervision of workers is one of the most valuable services an employer agency, as opposed to a placement agency, can give. The agency serves as your eyes and ears. It takes responsibility for the management of the worker as well as placement.

The alternative kind of agency is a placement agency. It finds a worker, but the responsibility for what the worker does is your job to monitor. They will also screen, and background checks their workers, but once the employee is placed, their role ends. The employer-employee relationship is between the aging loved one, and/or their adult child, or other relative and the worker. The person responsible for the elder's money pays the workers directly, keeps track of invoices, and provides either a federally-required W-4 tax form at year's end or a 1099 tax form for independent contractors.

Placement agencies generally do not assume the employer role because there is less risk of liability, and there are fewer complications to the job of providing caregivers if the caregivers are not the agency's employees. Agencies which act as employers of the caregiver have more risk and responsibility, and more expenses than a placement-only agency.

Who Would Find Out If I Hire The Worker Myself And Don't Take Out Taxes?

If you are hiring a worker to take care of the elder in the elder's home, then you set the hours and terms of work, and the worker is visiting regularly to do the job, the Internal Revenue Service considers the worker to be an employee, not an independent contractor. It is not likely that the IRS will come knocking on your door independently. It is certainly true that many people "get away with it," hiring workers in the home and never paying withholding taxes (as required by the IRS), never paying workers compensation insurance, and never paying unemployment insurance.

However, all it takes is one disgruntled former employee to contact any one of these agencies, and you risk substantial fines for failing to comply with the law. The fines can be thousands of dollars which the IRS assesses as penalties for failure to pay the employee properly and to pay tax money as the law requires.

Likewise, your state may require you to pay workers compensation insurance to any full time or part time employee. If you decide to risk it and not do so, and your worker is injured, and makes a claim for workers compensation benefits, it will then quickly become known that you have failed to provide this insurance. You can become personally liable for the cost of the worker's medical treatment, no matter how long it takes.

In addition, your state may impose a fine on you if you terminate your worker, and he or she does not have the opportunity to collect unemployment insurance benefits. If your elder has the means to provide home help, or you do, this is not an area to scrimp. The elder's health and safety are at stake.

For further information concerning the responsible use of a quality home care agency, contact the National Private Duty Association. This is the first association for providers of private duty home care in the United States. Visit their website at www.PrivateDutyHomecare.org or call (317) 663-3637.

Are Home Care Agencies Licensed?

Home care agencies are not required to obtain an agency license in every state. Some states require only a business license for anyone to provide non-medical home care services in an individual's home. Twenty three of our fifty states have standards requiring home care organizations to register or obtain a license. Because the requirements are different throughout the states, you, as a consumer, will need to determine if licenses are required in your state, and whether any agency you are considering using has the required license.

Be sure to distinguish between an ordinary business license, which anyone can get to open any kind of business, and a home care license. There is at least a greater measure of security if licenses are required in your state that a licensed agency will thoroughly screen and train its workers. Although even licensed agencies can end up with a "bad apple" of a worker, at least the screening process they normally use will improve your chances of avoiding someone with a criminal record, poor work history or poor suitability for the job.

Ten Tips for Choosing a Good Home Care Worker

1. Will help at home meet your aging loved one's needs? Think over whether getting help at home is the best way to meet your aging loved one's needs. Consider all options.

2. Do your research. If you are going to use an agency, talk to several, ask appropriate questions, and take the time necessary to do a thorough search for the best agency you can find and afford. The checklist at the end of this chapter is a good reference as to what questions to ask.

3. Involve your aging loved one in the process of getting help. Urge any resisting elder that you need the reassurance that he or she is safe while you are at work, or with your own family. This approach works.

4. Be respectful and courteous. Do not tell your elder how it is going to be or what is good for him or her. Be respectful, courteous, and ask before any decision is made. Honor the elder's need to have a feeling of control over his or her life.

5. Use a professional caregiver agency if possible. The risks of not doing so are tremendous. Ask questions, collect as much information as you can, and choose an agency which provides a lot of personal contact with the elder's family.

6. Determine your aging loved one's needs at the outset. Be sure a thorough assessment of your aging loved one's needs is

done at the outset of getting help in the home. An objective person from an agency can see things you may miss.

7. Be careful at hiring on your own. If you hire on your own, without using an agency, you need to do a complete criminal background check, a search of public records, driving record, references, and work history check on any prospective worker. Hiring on your own is not recommended.

8. Is the elder driving? If the worker is driving a car, be sure there is adequate insurance on both the elder's car and the worker's car, as well as a clean driving record and current license.

9. Monitor the worker regularly. Monitor any worker who comes into the home of your elder. Unsupervised time can lead to crimes of opportunity, whether the worker comes from an agency or not. Risk is reduced with agency supervision.

10. Remember to consider tax ramifications when hiring on your own. If you hire on your own, remember that the Internal Revenue Service (IRS) considers a regular worker whose schedule you set and whose working conditions you arrange, to be your employee, not an independent contractor. You must withhold taxes, report the worker's earnings, and provide a tax form according to federal tax laws. Under state laws you may also be required to pay unemployment insurance and provide worker's compensation, as well as payroll tax.

Questions to Ask When Looking for a Homecare Agency[8]

1. How long has your agency been in business? Can you tell me about the background of the owners/directors? (Many new agencies are springing up because of the vastly growing elderly population. Some are opened by people who have absolutely no experience or credentials to work with this population. Longevity in the business often signals a good reputation.)

2. What organizations in the community do you work with? (i.e. hospitals, Alzheimer's Association, Hospice, etc.) Do you have references in these organizations? Are there other references that you can give for your agency?

3. How do you find your caregivers? What kind of experience do you require of your staff? What kind of certifications do you staff hold?

4. *Can you tell me about the screening process they go through*? Are they background checked? Do you have them go through an orientation process? Do you have ongoing training for your staff?

5. *Is your agency employee-based or independent contractor-based?* (Very important!!!) Are taxes, insurances and worker's compensation handled by your agency? Do you pay the caregiver or do we?

---

[8] "*Ten Tips for Choosing a Good Homecare Worker,*" Hired Hands Homecare Inc., http://www.HiredHandsHomecare.com.

6. Will someone come out to do an initial assessment? Is there a charge for that service?

7. Tell me how the scheduling works? Are there any time minimums? Do we have to commit to a certain amount of service? What if something comes up and we need to cancel, how flexible is your cancellation policy? Can we expect the same caregiver each time? Is it possible to reach an agency representative after business hours or on the weekends?

8. What is your agency's course of action if our caregiver is sick or unable to work for some reason?

9. What if we have a last minute need, can you help us?

10. What is your agency's course of action if the caregiver is not working out?

11. How do you manage your staff once you assign them?

12. How does your payroll and billing procedure work?

13. Do you offer care management? Is there a charge for those services?

14. Please tell me about insurances that your agency carries. Are your employees insured and bonded?

15. Can the staff drive? Do they drive in their own cars or can they drive my parent's vehicle? What about insurance?

16. What can I expect the caregiver to do? What can't they do?

17. What can I expect from your agency in terms of communication?

18. Does your staff keep written care logs? How often are those reviewed?

19. How often will an agency representative visit my mom or dad to check on things?

20. My mom has Long Term Care Insurance? Do you work with these policies? How much assistance will you provide in filing her claim and assuring that all the paperwork is taken care of? Will you directly bill these companies?

References

American Association of Retired Persons (AARP). 601 E Street NW, Washington, DC 20049. http://www.aarp.org.

"In-home Care for a Loved One…Will You Gamble with Your Choice of Home Care?" 941 East 86th Street, Suite 270, Indianapolis, IN 46240. http://www.privatedutyhomecare.org.

"Consumer and Worker Risks from the Use of Nurse Registries and Independent Contractor Companies," National Private Duty Association (NPDA). 941 East 86th Street, Suite 270, Indianapolis, IN 46240. http://www.privatedutyhomecare.org.

"Ten Tips for Choosing a Good Homecare Worker," Hired Hands Homecare, Inc. 84 Galli Drive, Novato, CA 94949. http://www.HiredHandsHomecare.com.

Chapter Three
How to Understand the Pros and Cons of Assisted Living

Introduction

Because there is no single definition of what we sometimes call "assisted living," considerable confusion exists about it. Generally, the term refers to a place where aging parents live in a group setting, often with private apartments or rooms, and where they receive assistance with personal care and meals. The confusion stems from the use of the word "care" by assisted living facilities. For the average consumer, there is an assumption about what "care" is, when it comes to Mom or Dad. Many facilities are great places to live, as they provide many social benefits for elders who need some care, but want to retain independence. There is a blurred line in many consumers' minds about the differences between assisted living facilities and nursing homes, which provide nursing care.

This chapter of our series for boomer children with aging parents is directed at clearing up some of the confusion about what they can expect and should not expect from assisted living. Probably no one wants to live in a nursing home as a first choice.

Assisted living facilities fill a tremendous need for families with aging parents, and for our elders, themselves, once the need for a little help is clear to them. However, it is important to recognize that the law treats assisted living facilities in a very different way from nursing homes, often referred to as "skilled nursing facilities." The major reason is that Medicare covers some care in skilled nursing facilities, and Medicaid covers even more of this care. Both Medicare and Medicaid, being government funded insurance programs, have extensive rules that apply to these homes. Understanding how this works is very important if your elder is about to enter one form of care facility or the other, or if you are currently thinking about a move for your aging loved one.

Please consider this chapter an introduction to understanding the differences between assisted living and skilled nursing facilities. It is not a comprehensive study of every kind of assisted living in every state. Things may be different where you live. But, no matter where you are, your aging parents will get the most for their money (or yours, if you're paying), if you know what you are buying, and what the limitations are with assisted living facilities. I am an advocate for allowing as much independence for elders as possible. I am also an advocate for making safe choices for aging loved ones. I hope this sheds some light on a broad and perhaps confusing subject.

How to Understand the Pros and Cons of Assisted Living

There are no uniform definitions of what this term means, and the term "assisted living" is used differently in different states. Generally, assisted living refers to facilities, with services, in which elders are housed in a communal setting. For purposes of this chapter, **assisted living facilities** will be referred to as **ALFs**. In some states and locations, they are also called residential care facilities, congregate living facilities, continuing care retirement communities, personal care homes, retirement homes, or community residences.

ALFs provide a place for elders to live independently in community settings, with some personal care available. Most provide all meals, social activities and services, transportation, and assistance managing the "activities of daily living," which means walking, bathing, eating, dressing, toileting, and getting up and down from bed and chair.

Typically, an assisted living facility is regulated by the state, and is built on a social model for living, rather than a medical model. The state may license the facility to provide communal living, with services. What this means is that assisted living is not, as such, a medical facility with skilled nursing care available and doctors on call for its residents. Rather, it is a community setting supervised by trained staff that assist, as needed, with the "custodial," rather than medical needs of its residents. Medicare generally refers to custodial care as that care with such things as activities of daily living, which do not require skilled nursing. The terminology can be somewhat confusing to the consumer. "Long term care" is one way in which the Assisted Living Federation of America, the assisted living industry's national organization, refers to assisted living.

However, the specifics of what "care" is allowed and expected in a non-medical setting may not be clearly explained by the industry. For the consumer, the focus of assisted living should start with a desire to meet the elder's social needs in a communal setting. Independence is emphasized more than care. With the benefit of supportive services added, an elder without complex medical care can remain independent. If the elder has more complex medical needs than can be met by custodial caregivers, a skilled nursing facility might be a better choice. Some ALFs do provide a great deal of care, however, and the line between what a skilled nursing facility can do and what an ALF can do is somewhat blurred.

Some ALFs have a skilled nursing unit or section on site. It may have a separate license to provide skilled care. A resident whose medical problems increase would have to move out of the independent or assisted living portion of the facility and into its skilled nursing section at such time that the custodial care kinds of services became inadequate. In those situations, it is usually the facility director or administration which makes the decision for the elder about when it is time to give up independent or assisted living for a skilled care arrangement.

What Types of Assisted Living Facilities Are Available?

The assisted living facility is a relatively new category of residential care, when compared with "nursing homes" or skilled care facilities, which have been available since well before Medicare was put in place by our government. ALFs range in size from small group homes with shared rooms to private apartments in large, luxury settings. The Social Services department of a state may license such facilities, emphasizing the social needs of residents.

This is in contrast to a nursing home, which is typically licensed by the state's Department of Health, and certified by Medicare and Medicaid because it delivers health care. When a nursing home wants to bill Medicare or Medicaid for care it delivers to its residents, it must meet basic licensing and certification criteria which those Federal and State regulatory agencies establish. The ability to conform to Federal and State health care standards forms the basis from which such skilled facilities get reimbursed by these governmental entities for care given to their residents. The rules for and government oversight of a social care facility, such as an ALF, are far different from those which apply to skilled nursing facilities.

Generally, the residents of skilled nursing facilities are sicker, less independent, and have more complex needs that require the close attention and hands-on help of nurses. Assisted living facilities typically do not bill Medicare or Medicaid. Custodial care services are not covered by Medicare, regardless of the setting in which they are delivered. Both Medicare and Medicaid distinguish between care that is classified as custodial from that which is classified as skilled care. Possibilities for kinds of assisted living facilities are the following:

1. Board and care. Usually, this is a room in a private home or other building. Rooms are often shared. Meals are offered in a common dining area. Bathrooms are usually shared also. The advantage of this model is that it costs less than a private apartment and there may be more one-on-one attention to the individual resident in a close setting. Residents do not have the option of preparing their own meals.

2. Apartment-style, with hotel type services. This type of setting offers independence, though meals may be offered in common

dining areas. Laundry services, some social services, assistance with medications, and limited personal care may be offered.

3. Apartment-style with personal care services. This style of ALF may have a more comprehensive array of assistance with activities of daily living, may accept incontinent residents, persons in wheelchairs, and every kind of assistance short of skilled nursing. It will likely also offer meals in a common dining area, and may give residents the choice of preparing meals for themselves in their own kitchens in their apartments. Social activities, transportation to events and doctors' appointments, and supervision of general health and wellness are often provided as well.

4. Dementia care. Some ALFs provide specific units for persons who require dementia assistance. These facilities must be specially licensed in some states. The state may require a higher ratio of staff to residents, specialized staff training to deal with dementia residents, and safety precautions to prevent confused residents from wandering outside. The kinds of apartments or private rooms available will vary from facility to facility. Ideally, such a facility will have programs for memory care, secured exits, alarm systems to notify staff of resident whereabouts, and other visual cues to help residents with memory difficulty.

Various combinations and versions of the above kinds of living communities are available in different areas. It takes diligent research to make a consumer-wise decision about which is best for you, or your aging loved one.

How Do I Decide Between Assisted Living Facility And Skilled Nursing Facility?

A decision about where an elder should move when living at home is no longer appropriate or safe is a serious decision. One should weigh the decision very carefully, as moving an elder from place to place can be very hard on the aging person. Confusion, getting used to a new routine, new people around, new sights and smells, different food, and different stimuli in the environment are all factors to which the aging person must adjust.

The ability to adapt to something new may decrease with age, as most of us know. Therefore, it is important to look ahead at the elder's needs a few months or a year or two down the road, rather than simply figuring out what the elder needs right now. For an aging person in a physically declining state, an ALF which also has a skilled nursing wing, division, or building on site may be the best choice. One should seek medical advice from a physician who knows the elder.

If the aging loved one has unstable diabetes, for example, and uses insulin every day, an assisted living facility may not be able to meet his or her needs for increased insulin throughout the day; as assisted living, as such, has no skilled nursing available to assess the changes in such a condition throughout each day, nor to adjust the insulin dosage. Any complex, changing medical condition which requires skilled nursing assessment and action day or night may make assisted living an unsuitable choice. The elder's regular medical doctor should be able to assess the elder's need for skilled care and advise the family and the elder as to which choice would work best for an elder contemplating a move out of the home.

ALFs with sufficient staff, sufficient training, registered or otherwise licensed nursing supervision and adequate safety measures for confused elders may be able to do many of the tasks performed in a skilled nursing facility.

If you are considering an ALF, ask about their ability to provide for your family member's needs. If your loved one is incontinent, has breathing difficulty, needs around the clock supervision, requires regular nursing assessment to remain safe, or has a combination of illnesses which require frequent monitoring by a skilled person, be cautious about an ALF. If you choose this kind of residence, you will need one which is large enough to have a skilled nursing unit available to keep your elder safe. Without a skilled nursing unit on site, an ALF cannot deliver skilled nursing care.

State laws may prohibit a nurse employed in an ALF from delivering hands-on care. The nurse employed by an ALF may be limited to assessing and advising residents about their health care, and training staff, rather than actually delivering care, such as changing dressings on a wound. If you are not sure what a nurse in an ALF is legally allowed to do, ask the director or marketing person in charge, when you visit such a facility in your area, or where your aging loved one resides. Be straightforward in finding out what care that facility can give to your loved one. It will help you make the important decision as to whether you want to have your elder live there.

What Are The Advantages Of Assisted Living Facilities?

There are many advantages to assisted living facilities which cannot be so readily met in other kinds of living arrangements. First, this model provides for an elder's social needs in a controlled setting with trained staff. It can do much to prevent or counteract social isolation, a major contributor to health risks, both mental and physical. Many assisted living facilities work hard to provide a cheerful, enriched social environment with many choices for elders. The access to a director, caregivers, recreational and social activities, as well as meals in common is conducive to enhanced mental wellness.

Some facilities are bright, nicely furnished, and have attractive amenities on site. Some are in settings in with access to gardens, patios or other outdoor locations in which elders can relax, congregate, or enjoy good weather. Many elders' physical needs do not rise to the level of requiring skilled nursing. A skilled nursing facility for an elder with moderate care requirements may be too much, and too hospital-like. Skilled nursing facilities are more likely to have a hospital-like look, feel, and even smell than an ALF. ALFs do not necessarily give one the impression of an institution. Many skilled nursing facilities do.

2.***Assisted Living May Be Lower in Cost than Skilled Nursing Facilities.*** A further advantage of an ALF is cost. Usually, the cost is lower than a skilled nursing facility, though in the higher end ALFs, the cost of assisted living may prove to be similar or greater. Smaller "board and care" or "personal care" homes are typically less costly than nursing homes. Fewer staff and simpler day to day activities cost less than a larger ALF with a great variety of amenities and choices for the elder.

Since Medicare does not cover long term care, cost must be a consideration for anyone who can no longer live at home and who needs supportive care. Nine out of ten residents in ALFs pay privately. A few states have Medicaid waivers, which allow low-income Medicaid eligible persons to receive reimbursement for services provided in an ALF. But, the cost of room and board in an ALF is not covered by Medicaid. A low income individual could pay for room and board with Supplemental Security Income, if the cost of the ALF is low enough for this to be feasible.

2. ***You Can Maintain Your Independence.*** Another of the greatest advantages of ALFs is that they allow the individual to maintain his or her independence while still having access to help with activities of daily living. A caregiver's help with bathing, medication management, or transferring from wheelchair to bed can make enough of a difference that an elder can manage well for a time, without having to consider a skilled care facility. Some residents are able to remain in ALFs for the remainder of their lives.

ALFs may work with the local hospice and provide end-of-life care, an important aspect of planning ahead for an aging person. Some people are very satisfied and happy with the community feeling they get, the friends they make, and the fun they enjoy with activities available to them in this setting.

2. ***Feels Like Home.*** A final advantage of an ALF is that it is likely to have more of a look and feel of "home" than a skilled nursing facility would. Skilled nursing facilities must accept persons with advanced needs for care such as feeding tubes, IV's, oxygen, infections, chronic, progressive disease, etc. Therefore, they must have the equipment, hospital beds, nursing staff and physician presence to do the job. The level of skilled care provided will preclude many attractive amenities one would find in an independent living arrangement. Some ALFs allow pets, and residents bring their beloved animals with them. Pets kept by residents are less likely to be allowed in skilled nursing facilities, due to health regulations.

Some individuals live out their days in skilled nursing facilities because this may be the only choice for low income persons who are Medicaid eligible. Medicaid will cover skilled nursing care and long term care for eligible persons in these facilities. For those who can find a way to pay for an ALF, the general atmosphere will probably feel less institutional and medical than a nursing home. If given a choice, most elders would choose a pretty, well appointed ALF before a nursing home. An ALF is simply more appealing for many who can manage without skilled nursing care, and who can afford the cost.

What Are The Disadvantages Of Assisted Living Facilities?

2. ***Expectations for Monitoring and "Care" May Not Be Met.*** There are various disadvantages of this kind of living arrangement. One disadvantage is that the elder's or elder's family's expectations as to what will be provided may not be clear. "Care" is a broad phrase with different meanings for different people. The facility touts its ability to provide "long term care". The family and the elder recognize that the elder needs "care". Some consumers put an elder in an ALF because they cannot bear the thought of a skilled nursing facility, regardless of the fact that the elder needs more care than the ALF can deliver.

Although the ALF will try to screen carefully to be sure the elder's needs and the facility's level of care match, this does not always work. Families may understate the elder's needs; either because they are in denial about them, the elder is in denial about them, or they have inadequate knowledge of what is truly needed for the elder. It is important to remember that although a nurse may be on staff at an ALF, if the facility is regulated by the state on the basis that it is a social model, the facility is not licensed to deliver skilled care by that licensed nurse. In a medical emergency, the nurse would have to call an ambulance or paramedics to address the emergency.

2. ***Skilled Nursing Care is not Provided in an Assisted Living Facility.*** The only kind of facility licensed by Medicare and Medicaid to deliver ongoing, skilled care by nurses is a skilled

nursing facility. This important distinction may be lost on the average consumer, looking for a nice place for Mom to live. It can become confusing for the consumers because some ALFs offer dementia care, some have skilled nursing sections, and some do not. Some ALFs allow people who need a wheelchair full time, and some do not, and so on.

Therefore, to avoid confusion, find out from a combination of sources what your elder's needs are. Get a clear idea about any medical problems your aging loved one has after a thorough assessment by a medical doctor. You will need your elder's written permission to talk with his or her doctor about medical conditions and needs, due to Federal laws protecting one's right to privacy about this information. If you accompany your aging family member to the doctor, it is likely that the doctor will discuss the elder's condition with you, as the doctor can ask the elder if it is okay to discuss these matters. If you plan to call on the telephone, it is less likely that the doctor's office, or the physician, will give out information.
If your aging loved one is competent to give you permission, and you need it in writing, ask the doctor's office to provide you with the form (called a "release of information") for your elder to sign.

The physician is bound by law to conform to patient privacy requirements, and the elder's family can become frustrated by lack of information if proper permission is not given. Once you have a good idea, from the doctor, of what level of care your elder needs, you are ready to move forward with checklist and questions in hand to determine which ALF might work for your elder. Good ALFs will also require that the doctor fill out forms, stating what the elder's condition is and what the elder needs from a medical point of view.

3. ***Assisted Living Facilities Can Be Expensive.*** Another disadvantage of some assisted living facilities is cost. The high end facilities can cost as much as $8000-$10,000 per month, with extra charges for each kind of additional service needed such as help with bathing, feeding, dressing, help with brushing teeth, etc. In addition, some facilities require a one-time large upfront entrance fee, which may be $20,000 and up in the expensive facilities. The fee may not be refundable, so beware of making a choice too quickly.

In less expensive facilities, there is a cost for room and board, and there may be extra charges for help with various activities of daily living, though all are likely to be less than a luxury level ALF. One is essentially paying for all of the social activities, entertainment, outings, transportation and other amenities offered, as well as room and board, with the monthly charges.

The assisted living facility industry reports average monthly costs in the $1000-$4000 range, nationally. In many locations, the actual cost is much higher than $1000-$4000 per month. The consumer should ask a lot of questions about what charges are added to the rent for elders who need the assistance that assisted living offers. By the time costs are added for units of service for such things as help with personal care, the out of pocket expense may not be affordable. In addition, if the elder's health condition declines, more and more charges will be added for things the resident requires over time such as bathing, walking, help brushing teeth, etc.

What To Do If You Have Limited Financial Means

If budget is a problem, it may be difficult to find a reasonably priced ALF in every community. For those with limited means, the best choices are probably in smaller, home settings with only a few residents. This kind of facility may not have any entrance fee. The staffing costs are lower in such facilities, and they may offer fewer amenities, little or no licensed nursing supervision, and no luxuries. However, they can fill a need for a modest means elder who cannot afford a facility with the best of everything. Smaller assisted living homes may be called by a variety of names, so be sure to inquire as to what the ALF offers before you go look at it.

Besides the internet as a source of finding ALFs, geriatric care managers, hospital discharge planners, social workers, senior centers and community agencies serving seniors may be a way to locate facilities in your community. The reputation of a facility may be difficult to find out, especially if the family of the elder who is considering an ALF lives out of the elder's area. We recommend using professional geriatric care managers to assist distance caregivers and family in choosing the best facility for your loved one, or for yourself. To learn more about the benefits of using a care manager, see the "How to Find and Use a Care Manager" chapter.

The investment in a care manager is worth it, as it can save you many hours of confusing searching, listening to sales pitches, and feeling overwhelmed. Find one in your area at the National Association of Professional Geriatric Care Managers' website at www.caremanagers.org.

1. ***Affordability.*** Not everyone can afford an ALF. For those who are comfortable financially, and for whom the amenities are important, an ALF may work very well. Additional services, such as a personal caregiver aide or other assistant, can be purchased from outside the facility and brought in to supplement what the facility has to offer, should the elder resident of an ALF require more frequent hands-on help than the ALF is staffed to provide.

Because an ALF focuses on maintaining independence, elders who can no longer be independent may fall somewhere between what an ALF can provide and what skilled nursing provides. For those with means, supplementing care out of pocket to provide more attention and hands-on assistance is an alternative that can keep an elder in an ALF, rather than moving to a skilled care facility. However, the cost of this arrangement may be prohibitive for most. Furthermore, not every ALF will allow a family to bring in its own supplemental caregiver aides to address changing needs of the elder.

2. ***How Do I Pay for Assisted Living?*** There are not many options open to pay for assisted living. Most people pay out of pocket. For those who have a good quality long term care insurance policy, the policy may cover most or all of the daily or monthly charges. If the elder purchased a long term care insurance policy before assisted living facilities were available, the language of the policy may not address this question.

However, it is important to speak with the elder's insurance broker or a representative of the insurance company which carries this policy to find out if coverage is available. Unfortunately, many policies were sold in this country for long term care before assisted living was even considered and consumers find out, to their disappointment, that no coverage exists for ALFs. There is absolutely no uniformity of benefits available among long term care insurance policies. They vary from policy to policy within a state, and coverage available in one state may not be offered in another. Seek competent advice from an insurance broker who specializes in long term care insurance policies if you are not clear about what coverage you, or your elder, may have.

Paying out of pocket for an ALF can sometimes be managed by using the equity in one's home through a reverse mortgage. This chapter is not meant to be a primer on reverse mortgages. We do suggest that this option be considered, and that you seek the advice of a competent and knowledgeable attorney who specializes in estate planning before signing up for a reverse mortgage. The interest rates are regulated, but they are high, as are the fees associated with a reverse mortgages. As with any important decision, learn the pros and cons, and weigh them carefully.

What Can I Expect From Assisted Living?

A consumer can expect the ALF to provide what it promises to provide: a sense of community, a place to live safely, and supportive services and care. ALFs typically require that the resident or resident's representative sign a contract, agreeing to the conditions of residency and for payment of the fees charged. The elder should receive what the contract says the ALF will give. Some elders or their family members become upset with facilities because the care delivered is not up to the level they expect. Others are satisfied, and eventually adjust well to the environment. If you are dissatisfied, it is important to seek a meeting with the director of the facility.

Sometimes, dissatisfaction arises from the expectation that a staff member will be watching over the resident 24 hours a day. Although supervision of residents is essential, and staff is available 24 hours a day, this does not mean that a resident gets "care" 24 hours a day. Any elder who truly needs "care" full time probably needs a skilled nursing facility.

1. ***Ask for Complete Disclosure of all Health-Related Services.*** You should expect complete disclosure of all health related services and custodial care services available, and the cost of each. Some facilities break the services down into very small increments (sometimes called "care points") with separate charges attached to each. You should expect to learn, in writing, as a part of the contract, what the terms are for termination of residency, including transfer to a hospital or nursing facility.

The elder has a right to know what happens if he or she has a complaint against a facility and to whom the complaint should be taken. The facility should reveal what it is licensed to do and what it is not licensed to do. Since this varies so much within states, and between states, be sure to ask about what the facility cannot do, if it is not spelled out in the contract.

2. ***Is there an Entrance Fee?*** Ask if there is an entrance fee to reside in the facility. This is common in larger, for-profit ALFs and is less common in smaller and mid-sized ALFs. The financial arrangements to enter an ALF are not standardized, so just about anything goes. Some may require a long term commitment by requiring purchase of a condominium or apartment, signing over certain assets, non-refundable security fees, community fees, and other charges.

The contract to become a resident can be complex. Seek legal advice from an attorney familiar with this field to be sure you know what you are signing. Other facilities may operate with a basic lease agreement and the first and last month's rent, much as an apartment rental.

Be a good consumer and ask about everything. It is helpful to take your time to do research before you begin physically inspecting facilities, as the number of places available in some communities can be overwhelming. Many facilities have websites, photographs, and printed brochures, which can help you screen out which ones you do not think are suitable. A marketing director representing the ALF in a larger facility is likely to be the person showing you around. The marketing director's job is to show the facility in its best light. A good consumer will look beyond that to find out the details the marketing person may not tell you, to be sure the ALF you are considering is the right fit.

How Do I Know If The ALF I Am Interested In Is a Good One?

1. ***Government Regulation and Monitoring of ALFs.*** Unlike the monitoring of nursing homes, the state Department of Health, and Medicare and Medicaid, do not monitor complaints against ALFs which are not part of a skilled nursing home.

Again, ALFs do not bill Medicare for the services provided, as they are non-nursing and non-medical. They are regulated as social service agencies, rather than health care facilities. Therefore, it takes more work to find out which ALFs are the best for your aging loved one.

Our advice is to start with location. If your elder is giving up his or her home, it is very important to visit as often as you can. Especially during any period of transition to an ALF, family presence is a critical part of adjusting to a new situation. On an ongoing basis, the family will need to monitor the elder's functioning and general health condition, as monitoring health is not a mandate for every ALF. Therefore, look for a facility located in a place that is convenient for family to visit your aging loved one, if possible.

2. ***Ensure the ALF You Choose is a Good Match for Your Elder.*** Next, look at which facility is a good match for the kind of

person your elder is, and one that can best meet your elder's needs. If your beloved auntie loves to be outdoors, try to find a place with grounds, a garden, and places to sit outside in good weather. If Dad needs an ALF, and he is an artist, look for one with an art program, and places where he can enjoy artistic expression. If Mom would get depressed if she had to give up her cat, be sure to find an ALF that lets residents keep pets. You may have more than one choice in your community.

For elders with dementia, it is essential to locate an ALF which has a clear way of dealing with residents who have memory loss and the behaviors which are part of dementia. Because Alzheimer's and other dementias present special care challenges for caregivers, ask about the training and experience of both the director and staff in handling this kind of resident. Safety is a primary concern for all elders. It is of critical significance for persons with dementia, as they may be entirely unable to tell when something is unsafe. Wandering and getting lost are dangers, and a suitable facility will anticipate those problems, and have measures in place to guard against them.

3. ***Ask About Residents' Rights.*** Ask about residents' rights and whether there is a residents' council. Also ask how residents make their ideas and desires known to the administration. What choices do residents have? Can they vote on things? Find out about complaint procedures and how they are handled. In smaller, home-based facilities, the owner or manager may live on site. Observe how the residents respond to the presence of administrative personnel.

4. ***What is the Community Like?*** It is not enough for any facility to simply provide food and a place to sleep. The idea of a community is that the elder can feel a sense of belonging, as well as connection to others in the community. Look for an ALF which supports building and maintaining a sense of community among its residents. Structure in one's day can be a crucial part of both mental and physical health maintenance.

Find out what structured activities are available each day for the residents of any ALF you are considering. The philosophy of the directors and owners of these facilities will show in the number and quality of structured activities they offer. Ask about activities for an elder with your loved one's limitations, strengths, and weaknesses.

Don't forget about fun. Even very impaired persons with dementias are capable of enjoyment. A good ALF will offer its residents many chances to enjoy life and to have fun doing things in and outside the facility. The overall quality of life which the ALF appears to offer is an important part of any consumer's evaluation of a facility. Recreation should be a big part of any program an ALF offers its residents.

5. ***Price Is Not a Guarantee of Quality.*** Price is a major consideration, but a high monthly cost is not a guarantee of quality. Look beyond the lovely antique furniture, fancy amenities, and extensive menus to the frequency of contact by staff with your loved one. If an elder is a bit shy, is there

someone on staff who will take the time to draw the person out, and help her engage in things? If your elder has experienced a sense of loss, is there an empathetic staff person to talk to? Consider that your loved one could spend the rest of his or her life in this facility. Take the time to choose very carefully, and make the best move possible under your circumstances.

Once your elder is committed to an ALF, and has moved in, it will be expensive, stressful, and even traumatic, to have to make another change and start over. Do all you can to be helpful in the decision making process. The American Association of Retired Persons (AARP) (www.aarp.org) provides a useful checklist on its website. If you are shopping for an ALF, make a copy of the checklist for each facility you are looking at, and compare them when you have seen the ones you might want to choose. Look for the "Assisted Living: What to Ask" checklist for a thorough outline of questions to ask and observations to make.

How Do I Get My Loved One To Move When The Time Comes?

It is generally difficult to persuade an aging family member that the time has come to live in a facility, even a nice one. Of course, as with any change, it is important to talk with your elder about the possibility of change before you begin the search for an ALF. Involve the elder in the decision making process if he or she is competent to do so. Do your research and narrow the field down to a few. Invite your loved one to view them with you. If his or her stamina is limited, check out one or two at a time.

Ask your loved one's permission to talk about this subject. If you meet resistance, wait awhile, and bring it up again. Insist, gently, that you must do this for your peace of mind. Keep bringing it up. Enlist the help of family members, if you have any, who are willing to be present and give you emotional support in the process of discussing the move.

If you are in disagreement with other family members about a move to an ALF, there are things you can do to address this problem. See the "How to Deal with Family Conflicts about Elders" chapter for more information. Try empathizing with your loved one, rather than arguing with him or her. One can avoid argument by simply acknowledging the elder's feelings and not saying that you disagree. For example:

Elder: "I don't want to go to one of those places. I'm fine here."

Adult child: "I'm sure the thought of moving is hard for you."

Elder: "I can't do it."

Adult child: "It won't be easy. I'll help you pack up and choose what to take with you."

Elder: "You can't make me."

Adult child: "Let's not fuss about this."[9]

---

[9] Lebow, Grace and Kane, Barbara. *Coping with Your Difficult Older Parent: A Guide for Stressed-Out Children*, (New York City: Harper Collins Publishers, 1999) p. 54.

The transition can be easier with proper preparation, respect for your loved one, and taking your time to get him or her used to the idea. Many ALFs will allow you to come and share a meal there to try out the dining room. Ask to speak to a resident with whom your elder might identify, and have the ALF director or marketing person introduce him or her to your elder. A conversation with someone who lives in the ALF can be reassuring to your elder, and to you. If you are a family member, you may wish to speak to the family member of another resident also. Ask what it is like from the family's point of view at this ALF. It is essentially, a reference.

Find out if there are any complaints. If you are unsure, ask the director about how the complaints are handled. In summary, educate yourself as much as you can about any prospective ALF. Do not take the director's word for everything. They want to "sell you" on their facility. Be sure it is right for you from your own observations too, beyond the sales pitch.

Ten Tips for Understanding Assisted Living Facilities

1. Be aware that an ALF is not a nursing home with fancy furniture. It does not provide the same level of care that a skilled nursing facility can provide. It is a social setting, not a medical care provider.

2. If you are considering an ALF, find out whether it is licensed, and what the law of your state allows their personnel to do and what it prevents them from doing.

3. Understand that an advantage to this kind of living arrangement is a home-like communal setting with meals and some services. Understand that a disadvantage is that no skilled nursing is provided, and that it can be expensive in some locations.

4. If you are looking for an ALF for your loved one, do your research. This can be time consuming, as there is no uniformity among ALFs. Size, cost, services and amenities can vary widely. Use the AARP checklist to help you.

5. Be prepared to pay out of pocket for assisted living. Nine out of ten people do. Medicare does not cover assisted living.

6. Involve your elder in the process of choosing a facility, if possible.

7. Ask permission from your elder to bring up this subject. If you meet resistance, which is common, wait, and then bring it up again. Insist that the discussion is for your peace of mind.

8. Choose an ALF that can care for your loved one for the long run, including end of life.

9. If your elder may need skilled nursing in the foreseeable future, look for a facility which has skilled nursing on site in another part of the same facility.

10. Make an effort to match the kind of facility you choose with your elder's needs, likes, dislikes, and condition. Pick one where family can visit often and monitor your elder's overall condition.

References

American Association of Retired Persons (AARP). 601 E Street NW, Washington, DC 20049. http://www.aarp.org.

The National Association of Professional Geriatric Care Managers. 1604 N. Country Club Road, Tucson, AZ 85716-3102. http://www.caremanager.org.

Chapter Four
How to Choose a Nursing Home

Introduction

There is often a sense of fear and dread associated with the very idea of a nursing home. How many have heard from an aging parent, "Promise you'll never put me in one of *those places.*" We may promise, thinking that nursing homes must be terrible. We may never think far enough ahead to foresee that when our aging parents live longer than we thought they might, and live with disabilities, dementias, incontinence, and other conditions, that taking care of them can become more than we are able to manage at home.

We may never think far enough ahead to foresee that some aging parents will outlive their money and run out of resources to pay for care. We may expect that Mom or Dad's money will be enough to pay for someone to come in and take care of them 24/7, until we find out how much 24/7 care actually costs. We may think that assisted living is a great solution, until the assisted living facility says Mom or Dad needs more care than they can deliver.

When adult children face these and other scenarios, it may come time to find a nursing home for an aging parent to live in, as long term care is necessary. In those instances, it is important to be a good consumer. It is true that bad nursing homes exist, and that the nursing home industry has not earned a great reputation. There are many tools available to help you find the best nursing home available in your area, many of which are on the internet.

There are, in fact, so many tools and resources available to help you find a nursing home that it is easy to get overwhelmed with the amount of information. This chapter is an effort to help you find your way through the maze of sites and tools, so that you can go about your search for a nursing home for your aging parent in a logical and systematic way, whenever possible. I have reviewed several good internet sites with guides built into them and I point out the strengths and weaknesses of each of them, as I see them. These are my personal opinions only, but the opinions are based on my extensive experience.

My personal experience with nursing homes dates from my teenage years, when I volunteered as a "candy striper" (we wore striped aprons), in a nursing home. I continued this until I had enough training in nursing school to work as a nurse's aide, which I also did in nursing homes. Then, I worked as a nurse in nursing homes, doing per diem (by the day) work in numerous facilities, over the first two years in practice. As a public health nurse, we sometimes visited patients in the worst nursing homes, checking on elders who had previously been neglected. As a lawyer, I brought cases against nursing homes for neglect. My thoughts on safety in these homes, also called "skilled nursing facilities," come from the experiences I've had over years.

My message is simple: be a good consumer if you need to place your aging parent or loved one in a skilled nursing facility. Be vigilant. You can find out which are the better nursing homes and which are not good by doing your research. You will be better off if you take your time to do your research in advance, rather than waiting until a disaster happens and you have two days notice to move your loved one to a nursing home. I hope this chapter will help you make the best choice you can for your loved one.

How to Choose a Nursing Home

The time has come. Mom can no longer manage at home. She is not able to control her bladder or bowels. You've had help at her home, but even that is not enough anymore. The physical labor involved in caring for her is more than you are able to do. You are exhausted from being on duty 24 hours a day, 7 days a week. You had hoped it would never come to this, but you know you simply cannot go on this way. She has several new medications and you cannot keep track of all the changes by yourself. There is no one who can lift the burden of care from you, and you have to make the decision. Her doctor has been urging you to place your mother in a nursing home. You feel guilty, but you know you have to do this.

In another situation, you are a "distance caregiver." You have managed so far with visits as often as you could make them. You had a good caregiver at Dad's home. But the neighbor who sees your father every day, and the caregiver are both telling you that Dad is getting weaker, and they are worried about him. He has fallen at home a few times. You know you cannot go on leaving him at home, as it is just not safe any longer. He is a little confused, but he still knows what is going on. How can you put him in a home?

An alternative scenario is that your loved one's caregiver is warning you that it is not safe for her to be at home any longer. Your loved one insists on staying in her own home. You feel torn. Do you do what you believe is best? Or do you do what she says she wants? How can you make peace with the decision? You feel guilty either way.

There is no easy answer for anyone. However, before deciding what to do, it is best to arm oneself with as much good information as possible, to make a wise and safe decision. The more you know about nursing homes in your area, the better prepared you will be to start the discussion with your aging loved one.

Do not wait until a broken hip, a bad fall, or other disaster strikes before you start the work of looking into nursing homes. Doing a good and thorough search takes time. This is a very serious decision. You do not want to move your elder more than once, if you can help it. Moves are very hard on aging people, and adjustment to any new living situation can take time. Show your loved one the respect he or she deserves by biting the bullet and going forward with the search for information to prepare yourself for the conversation to come about moving to a nursing home. You will never regret being proactive. You may well regret not being proactive and having to choose a nursing home under pressure, when your loved one is in the hospital with only a few days to search before he is discharged.

What Is A Nursing Home?

A nursing home is defined as a place for people who do not need to be in a hospital, but cannot be cared for at home. Nursing homes have full time licensed nursing staff that provide medical care, nursing treatments, and therapies, such as physical therapy, speech therapy, and occupational therapy. Many are modeled like a hospital, with nursing stations, hospital beds, and medical equipment visible. A nursing home is not a "social model" for living, as an assisted living facility is. Rather, it is a licensed setting, monitored by the state where it is located, to give nursing care to those who stay there for the short term or who live there for the long run.

Who Lives In Nursing Homes?

Almost half of the people who live in nursing homes are aged 85 or older. Three-fourths of those in nursing homes need help with "activities of daily living" such as bathing, feeding, dressing, toileting, walking, and transferring from bed to chair. More than half of nursing home residents are incontinent of bowel or bladder. Dementia is one of the most common reasons a person needs to live in a nursing home. People live in nursing homes because their physical or mental condition warrants it, or because they have become impoverished by the cost of care at home or elsewhere, and they cannot meet their needs outside a nursing home. Another important factor which causes some people to move into nursing homes is social isolation, and lack of family or other support. The government refers to those in nursing homes as our "frail elderly."

How Do I Talk To My Loved One About A Nursing Home?

Your aging loved one is unlikely to admit the need for help, even if those around him or her think that it is time to be in a nursing home. You, the caregiver or family member, will have to bring it up. Respect is of the utmost importance. Ask permission to discuss the subject. If your suggestion is rejected, bring it up again, and choose a calm environment and time of day. Stay positive about the subject. Keep bringing it up until you are able to have a conversation. You are likely to meet resistance. If you are the caregiver, and you cannot carry on any longer due to the increasing physical or mental needs of your elder, be honest about your limitations.

If it is possible to involve your elder in the process of choosing a home, preview some likely choices yourself, first. Then invite your elder to view the best of them, if there are several to choose from. Listen to your loved one. Discuss all the issues he or she brings up, and do not argue about the situation. If there is severe resistance, seek professional help. Social workers, social service agencies, and professional care managers who are experienced in working with elders may be able to intervene and help you. Ask for advice. Resistance in moving an elder to a nursing home is not a new problem. Professionals who are familiar with the problem can be a very good resource for you for the transition.

For extreme situations in which the elder is clearly unsafe at home and absolutely must be moved, but refuses to do so, legal measures such as guardianship or conservatorship may be needed to keep your elder safe. If you are in that situation, seek legal advice. (See the "How to Find a Good Lawyer For Mom or Dad" chapter to learn more.) Do not wait until Adult Protective Services or the elder abuse council in your parent's area calls you or your elder is harmed by a failure to act. Sometimes, due to mental health issues such as depression, or disease processes such as Alzheimer's or other dementias, an elder loses his or her ability to use judgment. The decision making process is up to those who are responsible for the elder in those cases.

Where Do I Go To Get Information About Nursing Homes In My Area?

Fortunately, there are many resources available to give you objective information to guide you. First, allow yourself to stop feeling guilty. Generally, it takes an entire team of people, from administrators to dietary workers to therapists to nurses to nurse's aides, to manage infirm, incontinent, and dependent frail elders. If you have borne the burden that a team of people in a facility would normally bear, and you are at your personal breaking point, it is very reasonable indeed to allow yourself to place your elder loved one in a facility. You will probably feel better about this difficult decision if you prepare yourself for the transition by getting the best information available.

Do your research. There is data available from agencies such as your area Agency on Aging, and on the internet. In fact, the number of internet-based resources of information on how to choose a nursing home can be overwhelming. A general internet search is likely to lead to over a dozen sites from official-sounding organizations which offer guidance. Our review of popular websites on how to choose a nursing home is summarized here, with some tips on where to start and how to use the published information. All of the organizations which have websites also have toll-free telephone numbers, so you have a choice about how to do the necessary research.

American Association of Retired Persons (AARP)
Website: http://www.aarp.org

Start with consumer-oriented website information. Performance data, rather than advertising, is a smart place to search. Consumer-friendly organizations such as the American Association of Retired Persons (AARP) and Consumer Reports offer good guidelines. The AARP website, at www.aarp.org publishes a state by state guide to 17,000 Medicare and Medicaid certified nursing home facilities. You can search by your state, county and city. The guide also refers you to local resources in each state which may publish a "report card" for each facility. Some states provide information about the state's health department inspections, whether citations were issued for violations, and information about complaints.

Click on the section, "Long Term Care," which is under the home page of the AARP website, and go to "Guide to Long-Term Care." There is a brief section entitled "Starting the Nursing Home Search," which is also helpful. There is a Nursing Home Checklist, but it falls short of giving enough detail on how to research a facility for special needs such as Alzheimer's patients. Other sites have better checklists, discussed below.

Consumer Reports
Website: http://www.consumerreports.org/

This site provides state-by-state information on quality, well-run nursing homes, as well as homes you may want to avoid. Nursing homes are required to comply with Federal and State laws to receive Medicare and Medicaid reimbursement for their services. Both the Federal and State governments must inspect homes regularly to see that they are in compliance with the law. This site provides information about which homes were fined for being out of compliance. Fines for violations are a warning sign to the consumer. You should check out the history of any home you are considering to be sure it does not have a history of getting fines for poor care or other violations of the law. The information is on the website via the Nursing Home Quality Monitor. You may need to enroll online as a subscriber, but it is free.

The Quality Monitor ranks all nursing homes in a state according to scores received for standard quality of care measures in each home, taking particular note of "deficiencies" that would put a resident in immediate jeopardy or cause actual harm. Those homes that failed to make routine state inspection survey results available to residents and their families are noted. *Consumer Reports* reviews the three most recent survey results for a home to determine how well they are complying with Federal regulations. Homes are ranked according to their aggregate deficiency score, and homes that scored in the top 10 percent are rated as potentially good homes. Those in the bottom 10 percent are the worst performers. Do not choose a nursing home without knowing what deficiencies have been found there.

According to *Consumer Reports*, not-for-profit nursing homes are more likely to provide good care than for-profit homes. This is based on their analysis of state inspection surveys, staffing, and quality indicators. Similarly, independently run homes are more likely to provide good care than chains.

This site also lists an Eldercare Locator number (1-800-677-1116) that can be used to reach your local Agency on Aging. This resource can supply you with a list of nursing homes and contact information for the local "Ombudsman," who works in counties to provide consumers with local information about care facilities.

Another useful feature of this website is the section on how to read the form which provides state survey results for each nursing home the Federal Government inspects in its regular survey procedures. It is called the "CMS Form 2567," referring to the Centers for Medicare and Medicaid Services. The survey results are publicly available, as each licensed facility is required to publish the results.

Long Term Care Living
Website: http://LongTermCareLiving.com

The American Health Care Association at www.ahca.org, together with the National Center for Assisted Living at www.ahcancal.org sponsors a free facility finder service at their website, www.LongTermCareLiving.com. The site is comprehensive, in that it focuses on nursing homes and assisted living facilities, and gives useful tips for making the transition. The site also contains good background information which can be used in conjunction with a checklist. The checklist it offers is not comprehensive enough to serve the purpose of helping you choose between or among facilities, but it does give some useful questions to ask. Use their checklist along with others, to be sure you ask enough questions when you go to visit a facility you may be considering.

National Citizen's Coalition for Nursing Home Reform
Website: http://www.nccnhr.org

National Citizen's Coalition for Nursing Home Reform is a group which dedicates itself to improving the quality of care in nursing homes by empowering consumers and citizens. It is a group comprised of consumers and advocates who need long term care information. It has a political voice and seeks to influence public policy to improve the care of elders.

From their website, select "A Consumer Guide to Choosing a Nursing Home," which is lengthy, but absolutely worth reading. It provides detailed background information on nursing homes, as well as information on what experts to consult in your search. It outlines the cost of homes, family involvement, staffing information about homes, inspection reports, and the like. There are helpful "tips" and "cautions" throughout the article. These are practical reminders of what to look for in your research. One drawback to this site is that it discusses Medicare's website, "Nursing Home Compare" at some length, which seems to suggest that the website is dependable. *Consumer Reports* publication cautions that the Medicare website may not provide updated information and that you should not rely on it.

Medicare (Nursing Home Compare)
Website: http://www.medicare.gov

The official Medicare website, found under the U.S. Department of Health and Human Services' main site, (www.hhs.gov) has a search tool, Nursing Home Compare, which is intended to assist you in searching for a nursing home. It has many limitations, besides being unlikely to have the most recent information available at other sites. We find it confusing and difficult to navigate. Further, it does not provide information on nursing homes which are certified at the state level. The website does give you Medicare and Medicaid certified facilities that offer skilled nursing, as well as a "Resource Locator," which can guide you to other elder care websites. It has a broad range of information, going far beyond finding a nursing home.

One useful part of the Medicare website is a good nursing home checklist. Again, it may be difficult to navigate and find this. Once you are at the Nursing Home Compare website, navigate to the "About" section, choose "Quality Measures" and then scroll down the "Understanding Nursing Home Quality Measures" article until you see a link entitled, "Nursing Home Checklist." Print this out and use it as one of your tools to take with you when you go to check out nursing homes. Asking the right questions will help you decide on which nursing home is best. Protecting your aging loved one is the goal.

Medicare recently launched a new addition to its website, called the "Ask Medicare pages." This addition may be useful to answer billing questions, figure out how to get health information for your aging parent, and how to get help if you are confused about coverage. It also contains information about long term care options.

If you are proactive and do not wait for a crisis, read as much as you can from local resources, the internet, information available through your local senior centers, and books, if you prefer. Ask family, neighbors, and friends who may be in your situation, about local nursing homes which they know. An excellent source of information that could save you a great deal of time is a professional geriatric care manager. (See the "How to Find and Use a Care Manager" chapter for more information.)

Geriatric care managers are in the business of helping elders. A seasoned manager will know the resources in your community and can give you guidance on which nursing homes are the good ones and which are ones to avoid. A care manager's advice is for guidance.

The ultimate decision will be up to you. If you are the adult child of an aging parent or other relative, you will need to take your loved one's preferences into account. He or she may not have anyone else who is willing to take the time to help with the choice of a nursing home. You are the "indirect consumer" of the services provided. Your loved one is the direct consumer, but he or she may not have a strong voice, or may be vulnerable in the decision making process. You will want to take responsibility for the decision about what nursing home and when to move with the seriousness it deserves. No matter what the research tells you, there is no substitute for your own inspection of a nursing home. A home with prior citations is not necessarily going to stay that way forever. A home with no prior record of citations, or few citations by the government, is not guaranteed to be safe either.

After The Background Research, Then What?

After you do the background research and find a good home or homes to check, it is necessary to visit in person, and ask questions. Your first impressions count. Rely on how it feels to be there for some guidance. If you are uncomfortable the minute you walk in the door, because the administrator, marketing director, or other person you encounter seems unfriendly, pay attention. The facility "attitude" may be reflected in the care rendered there.

If you are met with a friendly person, use the checklist of your choice and ask questions about the facility, what your elder can expect, and the details of care your loved one needs. If he or she has dementia, find out about the care for persons with this disease. If she needs help eating, ask about how many staff members are available at mealtimes to feed residents. Think through your loved one's day, and cover of all parts of it. Work to find out if the facility appears able to meet the needs of your loved one, with his or her preferences, personality traits and the quirks we all have.

Ask to speak with a visitor, the family member of someone who lives in the nursing home. Find out that person's impressions of the nursing home. Employees of the facility often talk among themselves (not necessarily in English, however). Listen in on any conversations which take place in your presence. If they are complaining, what do they complain about? Not enough staff? This is definitely a bad sign. Observe how employees of the facility react to requests for help from residents. Are they prompt? Do they ignore the call bell? Notice how long it takes for them to respond to a resident's call bell.

Notice how often the maintenance staff cleans the rooms and how well they do so. In this era of "superbugs," such as Methicillin Resistant Staph Aureus (MSRA), cleaning of the rooms should be very thorough and very regular. Nursing home residents are physically vulnerable to begin with, and living in close quarters increases the chances of infection. Some nursing homes take everything out of the room to clean floors and walls. Others do a more perfunctory job, going around furniture. Observe when you are checking out nursing homes. Walk the corridors and make mental notes.

Danger Signs

The dangers of the worst nursing homes are too numerous to count. Published stories of terrible abuse and neglect have appeared in the media for some time. Medicare and Medicaid have lengthy regulations of every sort, but both governmental entities lack the resources to regularly inspect homes often enough to be sure that all regulations are followed and that all deficiencies found are corrected as the law requires.

Further, the government does not have the resources to fight every battle the nursing homes raise over every citation. Nursing homes which are cited for violations may appeal the citation, spend a lot on their lawyers to try to get the degree of the citation reduced, and otherwise make efforts to hide from the public the extent of their failures. The worst homes tend to have the same violations over and over again.

When you check the website of your choice to find out the history of citations by Medicare and Medicaid ("CMS"), it is a danger sign if a facility is repeatedly cited for the same violations over a period of years. It is also a danger sign if you know the history of violations, inquire about it when you go to the facility to check it out personally, and you are given a vague answer or no answer to your inquiry. The administrator should be able to explain how the facility corrected any deficiencies CMS found. Avoid facilities which do not or cannot answer questions about correcting deficiencies the government found and for which they were cited in the past.

On the other hand, good nursing homes do exist. Dedicated staff and a caring philosophy are possible to find. Be on the alert, in your search, for the things that are "red flags," suggesting danger to you.

When you walk the corridors, notice how many residents are alone, lined up along the walls in wheelchairs, doing nothing. If you go more than once and see long rows of residents who look as if they need attention, but there is no one around, this may also be a danger sign. Neglect is a persistent problem in nursing homes. It usually arises from the chronic problem of insufficient staffing. It takes a special person to work in a nursing home. (This is witnessed by the author, who has observed the quality of her co-workers in a nursing home herself). Some of the nursing assistants and nursing staff in nursing homes are dedicated, responsible, and very caring. It is their life's work to bring good care and attention to the elderly residents there. Others have a far less interested attitude.

Criminal neglect, assault, negligence, and other sad situations result. The facility has a very difficult job, as elders may wander, may be unpredictable, and have changing needs. However, it is their obligation to provide safe and sufficient care. Be alert to what you see on your preliminary visits. We recommend more than one. Drop in unexpectedly and see how it looks when the facility is not taking you on a tour.

Find out about how often water pitchers are filled by the staff. Dehydration is a very serious and dangerous problem in nursing homes, especially for residents who have trouble holding a glass, who have a poor memory and do not remember to drink water. Dehydration can lead to bladder infections, altered mental status, and poor skin tone, among other things. Those, in turn, lead to more serious complications. If you do not see water pitchers in all the rooms you pass or you do not see anyone ever filling them, it is a danger sign.

Find out what the staff turnover rate is. Unfortunately, the rate of staff changes in nursing homes is persistently high. There are many reasons for this including nursing shortages, low rates of pay, the difficulty of the work, the sometimes uncaring attitude of the ownership, which could focus on profits more than quality of care in some cases, and our society's attitude toward the very oldest members among us. It is a nationwide problem. If you are able to locate a facility with longevity of employees, including head nurses and administrators, it is positive. The primary caregivers are the nurse's aides. They must be certified and trained. Ask about the training, and particularly about staff turnover among the nurse's aides, also called nursing assistants. High staff turnover is also a danger sign.

Another critically important area to ask about is what measures the facility takes to prevent falls. Falls are an enormous problem for elders. Aging affects balance, as do limited vision, slowed reaction time, blood pressure changes, and many other physical conditions.

Confusion and poor memory may lead elders to get up without help and forget directions to do or not do as they are told. The facility must anticipate this and take safe steps to address the risk of falls. Ask about the measures in place and how often they are used.

Some facilities, in an overly zealous attempt to "preserve independence" fail entirely to use any restrictive measures to keep their residents from falling. This is not safe. Some elderly residents, in some cases, require restraint of some kind to keep them from crashing to the floor and injuring themselves.

In our experience, we have seen facilities err to the dangerous side of not using any restraints. Historically, restraints on elders have been *over*used, leading to injuries and even deaths from the restraints themselves. Some facilities cannot seem to get a balanced policy that permits the safe, medically approved use of restraint devices for elders who are at high risk for falling without overusing them. They adopt an "all or nothing" approach. Restraint of an elder is a last resort, but one which can save lives, prevent fractures and head injuries, and permanent loss of function arising from falls.

This is an important area for you to ask about if your aging loved one needs help with walking, yet has a tendency to forget to ask for help. Do not accept the answer, "We use a chair alarm." The chair alarm is a device designed to sound off when an elder gets up from a chair. It connects to the elder on one end and to the wheelchair or other chair at the other end. The problem with this device is that an elder can get up and fall in a second or two. Staff cannot get there fast enough for residents who are at risk for falls, if they do not happen to be standing next to the elder when he gets up and sets off the chair alarm. They are fine for people who are safe on their feet, but may wander.

Chair alarms can help staff know when an elder starts to walk away from a chair. They are not a safe fall prevention device. Generally, find out about the philosophy of the nursing home concerning use of restraints, particularly if your elder is dangerous on her feet.

Two other areas which may indicate danger signs to the observer are the way skin care and toileting are handled in the facility. Medicare and Medicaid have numerous regulations that require residents be kept clean, and that skin breakdown be prevented. Regardless of the rules, failure to keep incontinent residents clean and resident skin breakdown are also persistent problems in nursing homes. Ask about how often residents who are able to use a toilet are taken to the bathroom. Find out if there is a policy about this. If your elder is incontinent, find out about how often diapers are changed. Ask how often the resident is checked to see if a diaper change is needed.

Skin breakdown of an elder can occur very quickly. It leads to "pressure ulcers" "bedsores," or areas of open skin, often on the tailbone area, buttock, hip or ankle, which can lead to very serious complications. Skin breakdown has many causes, one of which is neglect of the facility staff to turn and move bedbound and immobilized residents often enough. Ask how the facility deals with pressure ulcers, and what policies they have to prevent skin breakdown. In your review of the history of citations a nursing home may have received, beware of any which mention "decubitus ulcers," which is another way of describing pressure ulcers, or skin breakdown.

If you visit an elder in a nursing home, you are unlikely to see or know about a pressure sore unless you ask, or check the skin yourself. People who sit in wheelchairs for hours each day are at particular risk if they cannot get up without help. The best facilities track how often each resident moves around and takes weight off the vulnerable, bony areas of the body most subject to this serious risk. A good facility will be sure your aging loved one is walked, moved, turned, or otherwise has her position changed every two hours. This is the standard for preventing skin breakdown in any kind of facility which gives nursing care to dependent people.

Making the Choice

Once you have done your research, involved your elder if possible, and visited the nursing homes in your area, you are ready for the decision. Consider the importance of your ability to visit often. Convenience is crucial, as your job as a family member or responsible person is to be there as often as possible to check on your elder's safety. Think carefully about which location will make it possible for you to get there regularly.

If other family members are also able to visit, aim for a location which will allow them to share the task of overseeing the safety of your loved one. If you are not in an urban area, or a suburban area with numerous nursing homes to choose from, you may not be able to decide based on the factors we discuss in this book. If you are limited to one or two facilities because that is all that is available, you simply must become the "safety police."

Do not rest assured that the nice people in that nursing home will always do their job properly. Assume that every nursing home has some risks, that no caregivers are perfect, and that you will need to oversee everything to be sure that Mom, Dad, or Auntie is handled correctly. One of the most loving things you can do for a vulnerable elder is to protect him or her from lack of care, or from poor care.

That means establishing a working relationship with those in charge at the nursing home from the beginning. Let the charge nurse and administrator know that you expect to be informed of any changes in your loved one's condition. Some elders have no one to visit them. It is sad to see what happens to them. I have no doubt, after working both as a nurse's aide and a nurse in nursing homes, that those who have attentive families, who visit often, get better care. It is important to be courteous and respectful to the nursing home staff, as well as to let them know that they are accountable to you. Once you place your elder in a nursing home, expect that you will need to watch over him for as long as he is there. Look for a facility which will accept or welcome your input.

How to pay for a nursing home is not addressed in this book. Much is published on this subject elsewhere. The websites we have reviewed all address this question. For those who have not visited the websites yet, bear in mind that Medicare does not pay for long term nursing home care. If you believe that your elder should receive Medicaid to pay for nursing home care, be sure to seek legal advice from an elder law attorney if you are unsure of how your elder can become eligible for Medicaid. It can lead to legal problems if you try to hide your elder's assets to make him or her eligible for Medicaid.

Ten Tips for Choosing a Nursing Home

---

1. ***Plan ahead***. Do not wait until a crisis hits before you look into nursing homes. Most of the time, the family can see an elder's decline before the elder does. When you see decline and your elder needs help with several of the activities of daily living, get moving and start your research.

2. ***Involve your loved one in the process***. Ask permission, speak respectfully, and seek your loved one's input, preferences and ideas. You will likely meet resistance, but you cannot let that stop the inevitable when a nursing home is the only safe choice left.

3. ***Get professional help with the transition*** if your elder is extremely resistant and unsafe at home.

4. ***Do as much research as you can*** to find the best nursing home for your aging loved one. Use the internet, books, and local agencies serving elders to get information.

5. ***Make the rounds of the homes you think will be appropriate***. Ask a lot of questions. Use checklists. Drop in unannounced. Pay attention to how you feel as a visitor.

6. ***Interview family members of residents of a home*** you think would be a good choice. Ask what they think.

7. ***Be a keen observer*** of what you see when you visit the nursing home. Listen if you hear staff complaining among themselves about the facility.

8. ***Pay attention to any danger signs***: history of repeated citations for the same thing, lack of water pitchers, unclear policy about preventing falls, lack of clear policy about preventing skin breakdown, and proper toileting.

9. ***Consider your convenience as a factor in the choice***. You will want to visit often.

10. ***Remember to continue to oversee your loved one's care***. Remember that no matter what the folks in the nursing home say, you will still need to be responsible for overseeing the safe care of your aging loved one.

References

American Association of Retired Persons (AARP). 601 E Street NW, Washington, DC 20049. http://www.aarp.org.

The American Geriatric Society (AGS) Foundation for Health in Aging. The Empire State Building, 350 Fifth Avenue, Suite 801, New York, New York 10118. http://healthinaging.org.

American Health Care Association. 1201 L Street, N.W., Washington, DC 20005. http://www.ahca.org.

Consumer Reports. 101 Truman Avenue, Yonkers, NY. 10703-1057. http://www.consumerreports.org/nursinghomes.

Long-Term Care Living. 1201 L Street, NW, Washington, DC 20005. http:// www.LongTermCareLiving.com.

Medicare (Nursing Home Compare) http://www.medicare.gov.

National Center for Assisted Living. 1201 L Street, N.W., Washington, DC 20005. http://www.ahcancal.org.

National Citizen's Coalition for Nursing Home Reform. 1828 L Street, NW, Suite 801, Washington, D.C. 20036. http://www.nccnhr.org.

U.S. Department of Health and Human Services. 200 Independence Avenue, S.W., Washington, D.C. 20201. http://www.hhs.gov.

Chapter Five
How to Find and Use a Care Manager

Introduction

Many people have never heard of a geriatric care manager. The field is not one which is licensed, so the title can mean just about anything. Because our aging population is increasing rapidly, and people are living longer than ever, the need for professional help with our aging parents has created a newer kind of worker. The geriatric care manager is usually a nurse or licensed social worker. However, there are many geriatric care managers who are neither one of those, and who have no license in any field. They may or may not have training in gerontology (the study of aging) or any other field. The geriatric care manager can be of tremendous help for adult children who don't know the resources a parent needs, or what is available in their parent's area.

We are supporters of the use of geriatric care managers, particularly those who have a license in another, related field, such as nursing and social work. Because so many families in the U.S. are scattered and adult children may live at a distance from their parents, adult children must rely on others to keep them informed about problems aging parents have as they age.

When a crisis hits, a geriatric care manager can get to the parent faster than an adult child who lives across the country. Further, the care manager can do a lot of preventive care for elders and can promote safety and good quality of life. Care managers should know trustworthy home care workers, good physicians, senior citizen resources in their communities, and should be able to refer adult children and aging loved ones to reliable sources of help.

The purpose of this chapter is to let adult children know what geriatric care managers can and can't do for your parents. Our hope is that adult children will be wise consumers, should you use this kind of service for your aging loved ones. We also encourage use of the care managers' website, to pinpoint which care managers are available close to where aging parents live.

How to Find and Use a Care Manager

Whether you are across town or across the country from your aging loved one, the need for help may arise as your loved one's condition changes. The elder's physical frailty, mental decline, and loss of independence are all factors which can affect your ability to help your loved one. For those who have no training in the care and management of elders, the complex matter of safeguarding one's parent while assuring quality of life can be too overwhelming to handle alone. Your relationship with your aging parent may not have been comfortable before he or she began to decline with age. Or, there may be the problem of physical distance, your own work and busy life, or your sadness at seeing your parent so frail, so unable to manage alone.

The difficulty of getting involved in your parent's or loved one's life at the necessary level can seem like too much for you. Whatever the reasons, it is important to know that professional geriatric care managers exist, that their purpose is to serve the needs of your aging loved one, and that this kind of help can do a lot to relieve your stress.

Many families in our society are scattered in different locations. You may be "the responsible one," in a group of siblings or you may be the only child. You may be the person who is most capable of making competent decisions. Perhaps you have the Power of Attorney and now must exercise it. You may have been the one your aging parent named as the Agent for healthcare decisions in an Advance Healthcare Directive. If you find yourself in the role of having to figure out what your parent or loved one needs, and do not have the background to make a clear assessment, it is a good idea to get some help with this.

A competent assessment by a professional geriatric care manager can provide a perspective you might never have on your own. It can fill in the gap between what the elder's doctor can do (checkups, treatment of illness, prescribe medication), what the family can do on its own, and what your elder wants or needs. Many people have never heard of a professional geriatric care manager (PGCM). You will not typically meet a PGCM through your doctor or health clinic. You will not find their services covered under Medicare or most other health insurance plans. At this time no license is required, and PGCMs are not monitored by state Departments of Health or Social Services. Yet, this kind of service can make a world of difference in what happens to your aging loved one, and how he or she is cared for. A PGCM can do a great deal to help you.

So, Just What Is A PGCM?

A professional geriatric care manager is usually a registered nurse or social worker, though some are professional money managers called "fiduciaries." The care manager can visit the senior at home, do a comprehensive assessment of his/her needs, evaluate the safety of the home environment, determine how to meet the senior's needs, and provide a written plan of care.

The PGCM should be familiar with all the resources in the community which are available to the elder. If you are a distance caregiver for your parent, for example, the PGCM can serve as your eyes and ears, and can keep track of your parent between your visits, reporting any changes to you on a regular basis. The PGCM can also hire and check on any in-home helper you or your elder loved one need, to help your loved one remain in her own home. PGCMs do not provide direct care themselves. Rather, they are the ones who can see that care is provided.

What can a PGCM do for you and your aging parent or loved one? Some of the things a PGCM can do for you include the following:

1. Make doctor and dentist appointments for your elder, and accompany your elder to the appointments.

They can talk to the healthcare provider about health problems that need attention, especially if your elder loved one is forgetful of the problems or has difficulty explaining them. They can report to you what happened and ask any questions you want asked of the healthcare provider. If your aging parent keeps telling you "everything's fine" after doctor's visits, when you know everything isn't fine, having someone qualified to accompany Mom or Dad to the doctor or dentist can be very useful. PGCMs can also provide transportation to appointments for those who have no other alternatives and who do not drive.

2. Interview, screen, and monitor in-home helpers, such as companions, aides, and other workers.

Getting a little help at home can assure that your aging loved one remains in his or her home as long as possible. However, the difficulty of locating a safe, honest in-home helper can be beyond the capability of some impaired and frail elders. The very reasons your elder may need help in the first place can interfere with his or her ability to get that help independently. For example, plenty of elders have impaired vision, hearing, and memory. Your mother may not use the internet. Your father may not be able to recall whom he spoke to on the telephone yesterday. Therefore, having a PGCM can solve the problem of hiring, supervision, and ongoing monitoring of the work the helper is doing.

3. Visit the elder when you want them to, even if you are unable to do so yourself, and report to you how your elder is doing.

Because there are many adult children who do not live in the same community with their aging parents, a problem arises when it becomes clear that someone needs to watch over the aging person. Neighbors and friends can be wonderful resources for out-of-area family members to call on to find out from an objective source how their parent is doing, but it may not be enough. Sometimes, the neighbors and friends are themselves elderly and less than observant of changes in the parent's condition. The best friend or neighbor may not be trained to look for ominous signs of danger needing healthcare attention.

A PGCM can look in on the elder on a regular basis, whether it is monthly, weekly, or what is indicated by the aging person's condition. A verbal or written report to you can be useful in making decisions, as well as putting one's mind to rest.

Unfortunately, guilt seems to operate in these situations. The adult child feels responsible, yet cannot take the parent into the child's own home for various reasons. Sometimes, the elder has no interest in moving, even if moving in with an adult child is better than staying put. A geriatric care manager can be helpful in relieving the guilt associated with "not taking care of" the aging parent. Perhaps, if the relationship with the elder is good and the time is right, the PGCM can lay the groundwork for persuading a change in the parent's living situation. Regular visits can do much to build trust, and trust is essential if a person must give up his or her home at the suggestion of another.

4. Act as an advocate for your elder at the hospital, assisted living facility, or other location where your elder may not be able to speak well for himself.

Hospitals can be dangerous places, as can other long term care facilities. The chronic, nationwide nursing shortage is no small contributor to the danger of being in a hospital. Unfortunately, about 100,000 people a year die in the United States as a result of preventable medical errors. If your elder loved one needs to go to a hospital, and you live far away, it is safest to have someone visit every day for as long as family members and friends are available. If they are not available, a geriatric care manager who is a nurse can do this task and report to the family members, until they are able to be in attendance or for as long as the family desires and can afford to have this specialized help at hand.

5. Maintain records your elder may need, such as medical, prescription, financial, or legal papers, and make them accessible to you when you need them.

If your aging loved one has trouble keeping track of paperwork, such as bills, bank statements, or other documents, it can create a serious problem. In our practice, one client's mother had been paying her Medicare supplemental insurance until she fell and was hospitalized. The adult child nearby could not find any organized paperwork, so she did no bill paying. The supplemental insurance was cancelled for lack of payment of premiums. The hospitalization generated enormous charges, many of which were not covered by Medicare. We were able to advocate for the elder and get the supplemental insurance reinstated, but it was an expense for the family members and the elder to pay for professional legal services to straighten out the mess after the fact.

It would have been far more efficient and less expensive to retain a geriatric care manager to organize all of the bills and monthly expenses ahead of time before disaster struck. Then, the adult children would have had the necessary information in one place when Mom had to go to the hospital, and the insurance premiums would have gotten paid on time, averting the cancellation.

6. Help you with the decision to move your family member out of the family home when the time comes, and assist with all the details of moving. Help you choose the right place to go.

If Mom, Dad or your beloved Aunt Jan is not able to manage safely at home any longer, she or he must go to another location which provides supervision. Locating the right place can be a very time consuming chore. It should involve visiting prospects with and without your elder to see how they feel to you. Reading the contracts, understanding what is involved in the move and planning ahead for the many details of moving out of the family home can be very daunting. A geriatric care manager can take some or all of the load off your shoulders. As someone outside the family, the PGCM can offer advice to the elder which may not be as suspect as advice from adult children in dealing with a parent who is resistant to change, as many elders are.

7. Provide information about social activities, safety, adult day health services, senior centers, equipment, transportation, meals, and other things your elder's community may offer to enrich and improve your elder's life.

If you live in the same neighborhood as your aging loved one, you may not need help with knowing how to find suitable activities for your elder. However, most children of elders have not involved themselves with activities for seniors and may not know the community resources or how to find them. Doing what you can to prevent social isolation can keep your elder safer physically and healthier mentally. A local PGCM should know how to find enjoyable activities for your parent, and can take him or her there to get acquainted if you are unable or not ready to do it.

What Is The Availability Of A PGCM?

The PGCM is typically available to you 7 days a week, 24 hours a day. In many ways, it is an investment in the safe keeping and quality of life of your elder loved one to hire this kind of assistant to you and your family.

What Are PGCMs Not Allowed To Do?

A PGCM is not a lawyer and cannot give legal advice. A PGCM does not give direct financial advice, though some PGCMs assist with budgeting, and household money management such as paying bills, and even help with selling the family home. However, a PGCM is generally not a money handler for the elder's estate and must avoid any impropriety concerning the elder's finances. PGCMs are not financial advisors or accountants. It is not advisable to permit a non-family member to have complete control over any elder's bank accounts, unless there is no family.

An exception is when no relative of the elder is in a position to serve competently as someone in control of the elder's money. In those cases, the court should be involved to assure that the elder with no family is not abused financially. That is done through a court monitored process called conservatorship, or in some locations, guardianship, which is covered in detail in the "How to Handle Money for Aging Loved Ones" chapter. The PGCM can serve as a "pay agent" for the elder. The PGCM can also serve as a financial Power of Attorney for a senior who is not competent to pay his or her own bills or manage money.

However, it is imperative that systems are in place to prevent abuse by any Power of Attorney handling money. A representative of the elder, usually a family member, must monitor all expenditures and review bank account statements, checking account records and credit card bills. A Power of Attorney for finances, in the wrong hands, is a license to steal. Unfortunately, this applies to family members, as well. The subject of financial abuse and how it can be prevented is also discussed in a later part of this book.

A PGCM, even if she or he is a nurse, cannot provide direct nursing care in her capacity as a PGCM. The "hands on" care is provided by others, though the PGCM may be in frequent or regular contact with the caregiver or assistant for the elder. The PGCM is not an employer of an in-home caregiver, but is a monitor of the caregiver. The PGCM can report to you, the person who is responsible for your senior loved one, about the quality of what the in-home caregiver is doing.

The PGCM who has a nursing background can also report to you about the observed effects of medications and the quality of care he is receiving from the physician if the PGCM goes to the doctor with your aging loved one. As many elders are hesitant to question their treatment or may lose track of which medications they are taking, a PGCM who is also a nurse can be a valuable advocate for your loved one and can provide necessary information to the healthcare givers, physicians, nurses, therapists, and dentists. A nurse-PGCM's observations about your loved one may be lifesaving and life prolonging. Regardless of background, a PGCM can alert you to dangers, changes, and things about your elder which need attention.

What Kind Of PGCM Is Best?

There is no one kind of PGCM and no one formula that is suitable for every aging person who needs a care manager. To be a good consumer, you need to ask yourself some questions. First, can I/my elder afford this kind of service? In some states, PGCMs may charge rates from approximately $90 dollars per hour to $125 dollars per hour. The national range of charges may vary from a low of $80 dollars per hour to $200 dollars per hour. If your elder loved one has the resources and wants to stay in his or her own home, this option may help you to accomplish that for your loved one safely. Some kinds of long-term care insurance, especially newer products available from 2007 on may provide for some kinds of professional care management in the home. Some policies of long term care insurance may even provide their own care managers.

Otherwise, care management is generally not covered by Medicare, Medicaid, or private health insurance, in most instances. It can be an expensive out of pocket cost, but is far less expensive than making a mistake, placing your elder in a care facility outside the home and finding out after the move, that you didn't really understand what the place required or what it was lacking. It is also less expensive than having to move your elder more than once. Good advice from a PGCM can save you untold grief.

Next, you need to ask what is the most obvious need my parent has at home? If it is for in-home help with companionship, shopping, cooking, cleaning or transportation, and you cannot be there to supervise the helper, a PGCM with a social worker background may be just fine. If your parent is physically infirm, has dementia, has a history of mental health issues, or suffers from multiple, more complex medical conditions, a PGCM with a nursing background may serve your needs better. The skill of assessing changing medical conditions, discussing treatment alternatives with physicians, offering recommendations about medications, and advising your elder about treatment is most likely that of a licensed nurse.

If your elder is able to manage fairly well physically, but is forgetful about paying bills and keeping track of finances, and is vulnerable to being taken advantage of financially, ask whether the PGCM handles money. Some do not. A professional fiduciary may be the person you need, rather than a care manager. Fiduciaries should be certified by the state. Certification may not be required where you live, but anyone who handles the money for another person should be very carefully screened and monitored.

Some care managers do all tasks needed, including paying bills for the elder. Ask, and be sure to describe to the prospective care manager all of the problems your aging loved one has without making excuses or glossing over the problems. A competent care manager will visit the elder and do her/his own assessment. A written report should then be made to you and the decision to go forward can be based on the report.

How Do You Find A Qualified And Experienced Professional Geriatric Care Manager?

A search in your local community is one place to start. A national organization does exist, and a check of the website will enable you to compare and contrast before you contact someone you might want to interview. The National Association of Professional Geriatric Care Managers (NAPGCM)'s website is at www.CareManager.org.

If you are a distance caregiver for your elder loved one, coordinate a visit to your elder with interview time for prospective care managers. As a consumer, it is imperative that you have a face-to-face look at the person you may be hiring. Do you feel comfortable with this person yourself? Does the personality and style of the PGCM seem to be compatible with your elder loved one? How accessible is the care manager? Does the skill set of the PGCM match the needs of your parent right now, and for conditions you expect to be ongoing, such as dementias?

If your parent is difficult, is the care manager equipped to handle such personality traits as resistance and stubbornness? If you are the responsible one for choosing this kind of help for your loved one, be a good consumer, and do the necessary homework. It can help your aging parent, as well as bring peace of mind to you. Keep in mind that with any kind of help you choose for your loved one, you have an ongoing responsibility to assure that the helper is doing the job properly, and as you expect. Stay in touch and pay attention. Do not assume that hiring a care manager relieves you of all responsibility for keeping on top of what is happening with your elder.

Finally, beware of any person you hire to help with caring for aging loved ones. Professional geriatric care managers are not licensed or certified by the state, and as such, there is no criminal background check, fingerprinting, competency requirement, nor testing to determine whether the person calling him/herself a geriatric care manager is actually qualified to do the job properly. Those who hold a license in another discipline, such as nursing or social work, are tested, screened and checked by the state to establish at least minimum competency for licensing.

Ask to see the license to be sure it is current. The state boards which regulate both nursing and social work may provide current licensing status online through the state in which the care manager is located. Ask for references and check them out, should you desire to hire this kind of assistant.

The National Association of Professional Geriatric Care Managers is located at:

1604 N. Country Club Road
Tucson, AZ 85716-3102
Telephone: (520)-881-8008
Website Address: www.CareManager.org

Seven Tips for Finding and Using a Professional Geriatric Care Manager

1. Figure out what you/your aging parent can afford. If the resources are there, think about the most pressing problems your aging loved one has which make it difficult for her or him to manage independently.

2. Use a national organization or local organizations to begin your search for a care manager. Review qualifications, hourly fees charged, background, and experience level.

3. Plan the questions you need to ask the prospective care manager at the interview. Does he or she handle money? Does she have social worker skills, nursing knowledge, or other special skills?

4. Find out by your interview what the care manager's philosophy is about. Is there respect and patience? Will this be a good match for your mother, father, or other loved one?

5. Pay attention to your own comfort level with the candidate for the care manager job. If you are not comfortable with him or her, chances are your parent won't be either. Regardless of how qualified someone looks on a resume, sometimes it doesn't "click" when you meet the person face-to-face.

6. If you are a distance caregiver, be sure the care manager you are considering is available 24/7.

7. Once you hire a care manager, remember that you have an ongoing responsibility to monitor what the manager is doing, to receive reports and determine whether this is working for your elder loved one.

References

American Association of Retired Persons (AARP). 601 E Street NW, Washington, DC 20049. www.aarp.org/.

The National Association of Professional Geriatric Care Managers. 1604 N. Country Club Road, Tucson, AZ 85716-3102. www.caremanager.org.

Chapter Six
How to Handle Money for Aging Loved Ones

Introduction

Some aging parents are fortunate and stay mentally sharp until the ends of their lives. Others begin to lose their memories, and eventually lack the capacity to make financial decisions. This chapter is for adult children, to help you help your aging parents. Failure to anticipate that memory loss, and loss of mental capacity that can happen to anyone, is a recipe for disaster.

For elders who have been high achievers in society, who have always capably handled money, and who have been successful financially, it is especially difficult to imagine being unable to manage money. Even for the average earner, independence about money is precious to most people. When it comes to mental capacity, there is a natural resistance to considering the possibility that we might not be just the same in the future as we are now. For this reason, many people never plan that anything could possibly go wrong with their mental faculties. When a sudden event happens to the elder, leaving them dependent, it is a crisis for everyone.

The point of this chapter is to encourage every adult child and every parent to have the basic documents on hand: a durable power of attorney for finances, and a health care directive, sometimes also called a "living will" or power of attorney, for health care. They are not difficult or expensive to obtain, and can sometimes be prepared by low cost or free legal services offices for those who qualify for these services.

There are few things more distressing than seeing a vulnerable elder being taken advantage of financially. When memories fade and capability slips, the risks of financial abuse rise dramatically. It is my hope in writing this that every adult child who reads it will take the time to have that serious conversation about money and planning ahead that every person over the age of 40 needs to have with every parent over the age of 70.

With legal documents in place, "just in case," you will have peace of mind. If a crisis such as a stroke or fall leaves your aging parent unable to manage money without your help, you will have the right to act on your parent's behalf, and keep Mom or Dad's life in order to the end.

How to Handle Money for Aging Loved Ones

The problems of aging are both physical and mental, and can erode a person's alertness, memory, concentration and decision-making capacity. Dementias, including Alzheimer's disease, slowly but surely damage the mental capacity of a person affected. Capacity is typically not lost overnight, except in cases of sudden, catastrophic change such as stroke, head injury, or the like. In many other instances, the loss of ability is gradual and one can see it progressing over time. Most of us need help at some time toward the end of our lives. Most of us who live to be "old" are not perfectly capable in all ways until we die.

If you are the adult child of an aging parent, be realistic. Your Mom or Dad will likely need you to step in and take over some responsibilities about money at some time before they leave this earth. Most people cannot handle financial matters without any help at all if they live to be very old, if they develop dementia, or have other age-related illnesses that affect their mental abilities. They are vulnerable to making serious mistakes, having utilities cut off, going into default on a mortgage, or other disasters if family does not take on the job of helping with finances. Scam artists are masterful at finding vulnerable elders and stealing as much as possible from them.

What Is A Durable Power Of Attorney?

Both elders and the children of aging parents need to consider one, very important legal document that will allow the adult child to handle money for the aging loved one. That document is called a ***Durable Power of Attorney***. Some call it a durable power of attorney for finances. These vary somewhat from state to state, but all such forms have some things in common. The document is essentially an agreement that the elder signs and has notarized, which appoints a person to act on behalf of the elder when the elder is unable to manage finances and other business for himself or herself. Some such documents are valid at the time of signing them. Others require that a physician or perhaps two doctors verify that the elder is no longer able to handle finances without help.

For families, it is legally valid to have the elder sign a Durable Power of Attorney document only while the elder is "with it" enough to understand what he or she is signing and doing. A perfect memory is not required, nor is it necessary that the elder have perfect mental ability. The elder who is about to sign such a document must understand what he or she is doing, and the consequences of losing independence with money, and other aspects of financial well being. The elder must be sure that he or she wants to appoint a person to be the agent to act as the power of attorney. It is important for those who have responsibility for the elder to get this document prepared at a time when it is still clear that the elder can make sense of it. Otherwise, it is not legally valid.

Having an elder sign anything when he or she is not competent is improper. It also creates a risk for the family member who gets a signature under such circumstances for possible charges of abuse. If you are not sure if the elder in your life is capable of signing such a document, ask your elder's doctor to evaluate him or her for this purpose. The safest way to get an evaluation is from a mental health professional who is trained to assess older persons on the question of mental capacity. A licensed psychologist, neuropsychologist, or psychiatrist has the proper training to do this kind of assessment.

Legal advice to prepare the Durable Power of Attorney (DPOA) document is very helpful because having a durable power of attorney has such an impact on the elder's rights. Properly used, a DPOA is a wonderful tool to allow a loving relative help a vulnerable elder manage her or his assets and do business safely and legally. Wrongly used, it is a license to steal. Every elder should have this important document ready before it is too late. It is too late when the elder can no longer think straight or make good decisions. There is no exact age when it should be done.

Although it is possible to get this document signed without legal advice, it can be dangerous, as it is necessary for the elder to be clear about what is to be signed; the wording of the document must also be correct and follow the law of the state where the elder lives. Without any advice from a lawyer, one could use the wrong document, the wrong kind of power of attorney, or one that a financial institution, real estate broker, or account administrator won't honor when the time comes to use it.

We recommend that everyone 60 years old and above get this document done and store it in a safe place with other important papers such as a will, trust, deed, or birth certificate. The aging person must choose an agent for this purpose to serve as the power of attorney. An estate planning or elder law attorney is the usual one to prepare the document. It is part of a good estate plan and is often done in connection with setting up a trust, writing a will, and getting a healthcare directive signed.

A lawyer should advise the person who is going to be appointed to be the power of attorney for the elder of his or her legal obligations and rights as a power of attorney.

If the Durable Power of Attorney is effective immediately, the agent must have the original document, and the elder should keep a copy. If the DPOA document is written so that it is effective only after the elder is determined to be incompetent in money matters, the original should remain with the attorney who prepared it. The elder and the appointed agent should have a copy. Once the attorney has proof, as set out in the document as to when it should be effective, the attorney will then give the agent the original, signed, and notarized DPOA document.

If the document says that verification is needed from two doctors that the elder no longer has capacity to handle money, two letters from doctors must be provided to the attorney, and the document then becomes available for the agent to use. The court is not involved in this process. The advantage of doing this without a court being involved is that it is less expensive and far less burdensome than any proceeding that does require the court's participation, such as a guardianship/conservatorship.

The disadvantage of no court involvement is that no one is watching what the agent or person with power over another's finances is doing. There is a risk of theft, financial abuse, and other financial harm to the incompetent elder.

When Is It Right To Ask A Parent About Signing A Power Of Attorney?

It is right to ask a parent to plan ahead by signing a power of attorney at any time, while the parent is still capable. A plan to bring up the subject should be discussed beforehand. After a holiday get-together, for example, is a good time, as family may all be together. An adult child may ask the parent to set some time aside the next day and extend one's visit to parents to include this time. It is important to bring up the subject with siblings or other close family members who may be available after or before a family get together to structure the time to discuss this matter.

Someone must take the lead. Sometimes it is the most capable adult child among siblings. Whoever does this needs to say that all family need to take some time when you are going to see each other to spend an hour or more planning ahead and talking about a Durable Power of Attorney. Incidentally, it may also be a good time to discuss the many other issues parents face in planning for the future.

For those responsible for caring for aging loved ones, it is a vital duty to watch the elder for signs of decline in mental ability. This does not suggest that everyone who forgets where one put one's glasses needs someone to take over as power of attorney. Some memory loss may be a normal part of aging, but forgetting important dates, such as when the mortgage payment is due, or losing track of time, and forgetting to take medication are danger signs.

A family member must be willing to take over the responsibility of paying bills, keeping track of finances, and managing all assets if the elder loses the necessary ability to do this safely. It can be a very difficult subject to bring up with an aging person. Loss of the ability to manage finances properly does not necessarily mean that the elder is "completely out of it."

Many older persons are very reluctant to admit to failing mental ability or failing ability to keep track of money. This may be out of fear. What will happen to me if I can't think for myself? It is easier to put if off than to face it. Many in our society are in denial about aging. Children do not want to face that the Mom or Dad they've always known is getting older, and getting closer to death. Elders, themselves, may not be comfortable with their own advancing years and getting closer to the end of life.

When Is A Durable Power Of Attorney Necessary?

Aging for many is a slow decline, and mental competency may not be clear-cut one day and gone entirely the next. For those who have aging loved ones, it is prudent to take the initiative to plan ahead and get the Durable Power of Attorney signed right away if you see signs of trouble. Chances are the elder will not cheerfully tell you, "By the way, I'm losing it. How about taking over my checkbook?" The adult child or other relative usually has to bring up the subject.

The help of the primary care doctor may be necessary to push the process forward. A psychological or mental health assessment can provide concrete information on which to base the decision to hand over the bookkeeping, the checkbook, and the banking, to the responsible person. An objective health care provider can test the elder for the capacity to make decisions, to understand, and even to recognize the differences between one thing and another. A diagnosis, test result, or recommendation from the doctor to let someone take over the finances can be helpful in having this kind of difficult conversation with the aging loved one.

Sometimes it is the elder who is realistic and the adult child who refuses to discuss what happens next when signs of decline are showing. If you are worried about your aging loved one and you get stubborn resistance when you try to talk about this problem, get help.

Some families avoid the whole subject of aging. Their style is to keep everything "private" and to act as if everything will stay the same for a lifetime. If you are in this kind of family, you cannot afford to let this matter of planning ahead go unattended. One person in the family must take responsibility for opening up the subject of planning for the possible future incapacity of an aging person.

Disaster can happen in a moment. A fall, a stroke, a heart attack can create a crisis. As hard as it may be for you or your family, take the first step by starting a conversation about who should take over if there is a crisis. Talk about what happens if or when the older person can no longer manage money. A person skilled in dealing with family conflicts involving elders can consult with you to give specific advice if you feel lost about getting started or have a very difficult or resistant parent. Mental health providers, some lawyers who work with elders, family mediators, and social workers from local community agencies or senior centers are good resources for this kind of help.

Having a Durable Power of Attorney (DPOA) in place and ready for future use is part of the job of planning ahead for anyone. Even if the elder in question does not have much in the way of property or assets, it is still essential that someone be authorized to act on the elder's behalf when or if the elder loses the capacity to make good money decisions. A Durable Power of Attorney can be written so that it is activated and valid right away, whether the agent appointed uses it right away or not.

Alternatively, the Durable Power of Attorney can be written so that it is activated when a certain threshold is reached, such as when two doctors determine that the elder is incompetent. If the elder in your family is reluctant to sign over a power of attorney document, it may be easier for her or him if the document is not activated until two mental health professionals say it is time. The elder may feel more in control if you do it that way. The disadvantage of this is that it will require two doctor's visits, which may or may not be paid for by Medicare or any other insurance.

It may also take time if the DPOA document specifies that a doctor or doctors have to decide if your aging parent needs the agent to take over handling the finances. If the elder is suddenly incapacitated by a heart attack or stroke, and cannot get out, arranging such visits from mental health professionals can be difficult. Without a properly signed DPOA, the family would have to wait for these arrangements to conduct any financial business for the elder, such as writing a check, making a bank withdrawal, or the like.

It is sometimes confusing and difficult for the treating medical doctors to make the decision about whether someone is competent about money or not. The cardiologist, internist, or other primary care doctors generally do not observe their patients making money decisions. They may rely on family to advise them of the elder's status about this decision-making ability. Or, they might refer the elder for further evaluation by a psychologist or psychiatrist. This can take time and can be costly.

A full neuropsychological examination with testing and a written report, for example, can cost $1500-$3000. This kind of assessment is not usually covered by insurance and may have to be paid out of pocket. There may be exceptions, but it should not be assumed that there will be insurance for such an evaluation for the purpose of deciding if someone is competent to handle money. For this reason, some lawyers advise their clients to have the DPOA active immediately upon signing. It does not mean that the DPOA should be put to use right away. Rather, it is instantly ready when needed for any unpredictable situation in which the elder cannot handle finances.

Who Should Be Chosen To Be The Durable Power Of Attorney?

The elder's agent or power of attorney should be someone the elder knows, if possible. Independent individuals are employed to do this for people who have no family or no one who is suitable to handle their money. A family member often fills the role. If a crisis comes, and the elder is mentally incapacitated, someone must be able to sign documents and write checks during the period of incapacity, whether temporary or permanent. Elders must fully trust the adult child, friend, or agent they appoint to be their "attorney in fact," as the opportunity to abuse this position of power is clearly there.

We usually advise elders not to appoint multiple family members to be power of attorney simultaneously. It can be a breeding ground for ugly family disputes when one sibling disagrees with what the other is doing for Mom or Dad. Two people can share the responsibility if they get along and agree on what the aging parent wants or would have wanted if he or she was able to say. One person needs to be in charge. Ideally, the power of attorney adult child seeks input and help from adult siblings, though this is not always the way it works in the real world.

What Makes A Power Of Attorney "Durable"?

The "durable" designation signifies that the power of attorney has authority to make money decisions for the rest of a person's life. What also makes a Power of Attorney document "durable" is that it cannot later be revoked by the aging person after the elder suffers mental decline and needs help. We never know when this will happen. It makes good sense to get the document prepared while the elder is fully in control of his or her mind and able to handle money matters.

This is one area where procrastination about getting this document prepared can create an expensive mess down the road. A sudden stroke or other incident can cause it to be too late for an elder to sign the paperwork, and it can happen without warning, and in an instant. If an incompetent elder does not have a DPOA for finances and needs help, the court may have to get involved in appointing someone to serve as a guardian, also called a conservator. This is an unnecessary expense for most families. It can be avoided with a basic amount of planning ahead.

Can A Person Change Her Mind About Who Is Appointed As The Agent?

Sometimes, yes, you can change your mind. While the DPOA document is not activated, and while the elder *still has legal capacity* to make money and other important decisions, he or she can take back or change the DPOA. This can legitimately be done <u>only</u> if the elder is generally legally competent to make such a decision, knowing full well why the first person appointed as the agent is no longer safe or desirable to have in that position. The elder who had a lawyer prepare the DPOA should contact that lawyer or other elder law attorney of choice, and request the change.

The lawyer will make a determination that the elder is still competent, or the lawyer may request a mental capacity evaluation by a psychologist or psychiatrist. It is crucial to get a mental health assessment before changing a DPOA for finances to avoid controversy later on. Anything can happen, even in the space of a few hours. If a change is needed, plan it carefully, seek legal and medical advice, and act promptly.

For example, if Grandma decides her oldest son should be the "attorney in fact" one day, but changes her mind the next day, deciding her daughter would do a better job, Grandma can ask her lawyer to destroy the first Durable Power of Attorney document, let her son know that she changed her mind, and have another document drawn up at that time, appointing her daughter. Perhaps her son has been arrested for a crime or she just found out he has a drug problem. Grandma is worried that he will not be able to help when the time comes.

A person with mental health instability, drug, alcohol, or criminal history should not normally be given the authority to handle someone else's money as a DPOA. Grandma should see her doctor who gives her a letter verifying that she is still capable of making money decisions. She sees the lawyer who prepared the original document and explains why she wants a different agent now. The lawyer reviews the mental health assessment from the doctor, prepares a new DPOA, and Grandma's daughter then becomes the agent for the DPOA.

Why Do I Need An Attorney To Prepare The Document?

It is always advisable to have the DPOA drawn up by an attorney. Questions about whether the elder was actually competent to make the decision about whom to appoint as the agent or "attorney in fact" can lead to bitter, destructive, and expensive court battles. An attorney working in the area of elder law is normally capable of deciding whether the elder in question has the mental capacity to make this important decision about giving someone else power of attorney. If it is not clear, because there is some loss of mental ability on the part of the elder, but the elder can still make some decisions, the lawyer should also have the elder evaluated by a mental health provider to assess mental capacity to sign.

The record created by the psychologist or psychiatrist in assessing the elder will protect him or her later if the DPOA is challenged by a family member who questions the elder's ability to decide. It is possible to get the DPOA document prepared at low cost or no cost through seniors' legal services centers, legal aid clinics, or other legal offices which serve low income and elderly persons.

Some have volunteer attorneys who do this work at no charge. The America Association of Retired Persons (AARP) at www.aarp.org has a panel of attorneys who work at reduced rates for those with limited incomes.

Family Conflicts

Changing one's mind about who should be appointed can also lead to conflicts in the family or with the person who was "fired" from being appointed at first. Following legal advice can help avoid these battles. The role of money handler is a powerful one. Power struggles are part of the human condition. It is best to do everything possible to avert the family power struggle by asking your elder to seek legal advice about the Durable Power of Attorney, considering who is the best person to serve as the agent for the elder. Think about the person who is best in the family about handling money and taking on the responsibility of keeping track of it.

It need not be a family member if none are available or suitable for the job. A friend or other trusted person can serve as an agent. Think about the most honest and fair person who is willing, local, and available. This person may end up deciding where the elder is going to live, when the family home should be sold, how much the elder should have as a living allowance, and all other money decisions.

It is illegal to get an elder who does not understand the consequences of appointing a power of attorney agent to sign a DPOA or change the name of the agent later on. It could be interpreted as criminal financial elder abuse to manipulate an impaired elder into signing anything he or she is no longer capable of understanding. Financial abuse laws are both criminal and civil. Those found guilty of the crime of financial elder abuse can go to jail if convicted. They may also be forced to pay back any amounts illegally taken from an elder.

What Happens If The Agent Is Financially Abusing The Elder?

If the agent serving as DPOA is financially harming the elder, and others are aware of this, the court would have to be involved in preventing further abuse. A Durable Power of Attorney is normally permanent, unless the agent cannot serve or wishes to name someone else to take over the job. If the person serving as power of attorney needs to be removed because of abuse, neglecting his or her duties, or dishonesty, drastic steps must be taken. The only alternative at that time, with an incompetent elder, is to seek court appointment of a guardian or conservator, with specific permission from the court to displace the poorly performing power of attorney previously chosen. Financial abuse should also be reported to the criminal authorities in the county where the financial abuse is taking place.

A guardian or conservator is monitored regularly by the court in the place where he or she is appointed, and there is therefore a checks and balances system to prevent abuse. Unless a family member or person in authority challenges an appointed power of attorney in court, or the agent resigns, the appointment of a DPOA lasts from the time it is activated to the end of the elder's life. If a friend, family member or other who cares about the elder notices signs of a power of attorney abusing the role and misusing the elder's money, it is urgent that the local Adult Protective Services, police, or district attorney be contacted to report the suspected abuse immediately. As mentioned, a DPOA in the wrong hands can become a license to steal, and it can be difficult to stop.

What Else Should I Do To Plan Ahead In Case My Parent Becomes Incapacitated?

Anticipate that most of us decline with age. Get information from your aging loved ones. Which bank does she use? Where is the mortgage, the deed to the home, the checkbook? Are there investments? How is Social Security received? Aids to help you organize your aging parents' or other loved one's financial information is available from many sources. A simple binder, computer record, or list will do. Be thorough and be sure you know where all the financial resources are and what they are.

Your aging elder may feel that his or her privacy is being invaded by your nosy questions, but you have no choice. It is better to risk being called nosy and to get the necessary information than to get an emergency call that Mom or Dad is in the hospital, and you have no idea where to find their financial data when you need it. Bills will come in, mortgage payments will be due, and other obligations of an incapacitated parent continue. If the elder cannot speak or is in a coma, how will you find out what you need to know? If the prospect of the difficult conversation overwhelms you and stops you, it makes sense to get support, guidance and direction from a professional.

If you are signing another person's name without a DPOA or court appointment as a guardian/conservator, it is a criminal offense. Verbal permission to sign your mother's or father's name for her or him is not enough. Signing someone else's name on any legal document, including a check, without the person's notarized signature on a power of attorney document (unless you are a guardian or conservator) is forgery. Forgery is a crime in every state. Therefore, a family member or friend wishing to help must have a signed, notarized Durable Power of Attorney to do money related business for an aging loved one.

The person acting in the capacity of power of attorney is normally given the authority to go considerably further than simply making money decisions. The document giving authority often includes the power to decide where the elder should live, what help should be hired, how to preserve quality of life for the elder, and how all the assets of the elder should be spent. Conceivably, a power of attorney could place the elder in a nursing home, assisted living facility, or board and care home, as the agent has sole authority to make all financial decisions without permission from anyone else. The power of attorney can force the elder to stay in a place he or she does not like, even if there is no financial abuse involved. Making the right choice for this important agent job has far reaching consequences.

To adequately plan ahead for your aging parent, have the conversation, get the documents you need prepared, and know where the elder's assets are. It is very useful to ask your aging loved one about his or her preferences, and how the elder would like to have things done if he or she is incapacitated. It helps to have your aging loved one write this out for you, as the potential caregiver in the future.

When Should The Power Of Attorney Appointed To Serve Actually Start Doing This?

An aging parent needs to have someone serve as power of attorney at the point when the elder, the elder's family, and her or his treating doctor agree that help is necessary. Sudden changes, such as a disabling fall, can make this decision easy. However, when the mental changes of aging are not sudden, the elder and the family members may need to get an outside opinion. If the elder is unwilling to be formally evaluated for mental ability, the elder's family members and doctor should confer to determine whether the doctor's routine medical examination gives the doctor enough information to recommend that the elder give up the responsibility for managing money. When all the "red flags" are there telling the family that the elder is in real financial danger and the elder refuses any help or will not discuss the subject, drastic measures may be necessary.

Leaving the situation alone when you are well aware that your aging parent is unsafe with money decisions is both risky and irresponsible. Financial abuse in our country is a huge problem, estimated to cost elders and their families $40 billion dollars a year. Don't let your stubborn aging parent become vulnerable to predators because he or she refuses to admit a problem. You will need professional advice and help if your parent thinks he or she is fine, but you are sure he or she is not.

Guardians and Conservators

A confused elder, an elder who loses track of things is a vulnerable elder. Legal means exist to protect elders in this situation, when they are at risk, are being subjected to financial abuse, or will not allow families to help them. The courts do step in with these extreme cases. A **conservatorship**, also called **guardianship** in most states, should be requested in court to protect the elder from financial disaster. This can be done without the consent of the elder.

Because of the heavy and sometimes irreparable harm such a move can do to family relationships, use of a guardianship for an elder who resists this total loss of financial independence should only be done in extreme circumstances after all other efforts at financially protecting the elder have failed. The elder has to be a danger to himself, and the evidence the court needs to take away financial freedom is significant. This is discussed further in the next section.

Warning Signs That Your Aging Loved One Needs Help Handling Money

Occasionally, an elder will request help from a trusted other person when she or he senses that he is not able to handle money any longer. However, it is more common for the elder to resist allowing this kind of help. If fact, most of us do not want to face the reality of losing our independent ability to make money decisions. Many elders are in denial about the loss of memory that can erode their safety around money handling.

Imagine never being able to write a check again and never being able to freely choose how to spend money, without having to have someone overseeing us. It is not surprising that this entire area is fraught with difficulty. Money is very symbolic for most people and loss of independence about money can be upsetting, depressing, and threatening for an elder. Loss of control over money can symbolize loss of control over life and loss of freedom.

Even though the subject is difficult, it is critical to be on the alert for common danger signs that an elder is "slipping" and needs someone to step in and take over with money. Some warning signs include:

1. The elder has forgotten to pay an important bill and you notice collection letters in the elder's mail or bill collectors call on the phone when you visit.

2. The elder has neglected a part of daily life, which she or he has always attended to in the past. Forgetting housekeeping, neglecting personal grooming, not maintaining the yard, not putting gas in the car, or other forgetting can alert you to the fact that something has changed from what was usual.

3. The elder forgets that you were coming to visit, even though you called with a reminder just before the visit.

4. Marked weight gain or loss, which can be a sign of depression or other mental health or physical problem.

5. The elder is spending money on things he or she does not need and normally would not want. Odd-appearing changes in spending habits can be a sign of loss of ability to make safe decisions.

6. The elder is getting telephone calls and items in the mail asking for money and he or she is inclined to write a check or give money to all of them.

7. The elder gives personal information to strangers on the telephone or at the door, sometimes including bank accounts or credit card information.

8. The elder has made a new "friend" who calls or visits often, and whom you find out has persuaded the elder to give money to him.

9. The elder is isolated, has limited transportation, and has a lack of social networks from which to draw companionship.

10. The elder has recently lost a spouse.

All of these warning signs, and more, can suggest that the elder is vulnerable to financial loss or abuse. It is necessary to attend to any of these warning signs and act quickly. Financial abuse of elders is ruthless, shocking, and prevalent. The best way to protect your aging loved one is to handle all money for him or her, under the legal permission of the DPOA.

Another option is to have another family member or friend appointed to the position of power of attorney. The DPOA document should contain language that permits the power of attorney appointed by the elder to appoint a successor (substitute) in case he or she cannot serve or does not want to do so when the time comes.

Finally, one can hire a professional, called a fiduciary, to do the job. The professional may be a part of the state office of the Public Guardian or can be a private person who has solid experience handling money. Unfortunately, fiduciaries are not licensed in most places, so it is important to choose a reputable person by checking out his or her credentials and references. Some states require certification. Others have no formal requirements. Otherwise, the court can impose a conservatorship/guardianship and appoint a Public Guardian if no one in the family and no friend can or will serve.

The Duties Of Handling Money For Another Person

The responsibility for handling the money affairs of another person is a serious one, and it carries with it a heavy legal duty. Any person who acts on behalf of another in a position of trust can be called a "fiduciary," which is a legal term (pronounced "fuh-du-she-air-ee").

If the court in a guardianship proceeding needs to appoint someone to take over handling money for another, that person has a legal obligation to do what is best for the elder. The person appointed is normally a relative. Sometimes the person in a position of trust is a friend. Sometimes, it is a perfect stranger if no relative or friend can serve.

The fiduciary, guardian, or power of attorney is required by law to use the elder's money for the elder's benefit, and not for the guardian's benefit. This is true whether the money-handling person is court-appointed or not. He or she cannot spend the elder's money foolishly such as gambling with it, making risky investments, or loaning it to a person who has no interest in helping the elder. Whether the agent is a power of attorney, court-appointed guardian, fiduciary, relative or friend, the obligation to protect the elder's finances and use them ethically is the same.

What Can A Person With Power Of Attorney Do?

The person with power of attorney may pay bills, open, close and manage bank and stock accounts, buy and sell property including the elder's residence, invest money, or withdraw money from investments, pay for care or services, decide on which living situation is best for an elder, place the elder in a care facility or nursing home, and otherwise make all important decisions except health related decisions.

The elder may no longer have any say in money decisions if he or she has reached the point when a power of attorney is necessary. The law builds in the basic protection of having a formal document in place and requiring a notary public to verify the signature to protect against someone using another's identity. Unfortunately, the Durable Power of Attorney document itself does not protect the elder against the wrong use of the document, nor does it have any connection to the courts. It allows virtually unlimited freedom to make money decisions.

There is no legal requirement that a power of attorney be related to the elder. It is certainly a problem for those who have no children or other relatives to choose someone trustworthy. Very sad cases of financial abuse have occurred when the former secretary, housekeeper, gardener, or other person close to the elder was given a Durable Power of Attorney. It is truly a "license to steal" in the hands of an unscrupulous person whose motive is to take the elder's money. Even those who have known the elder for many years are not necessarily trustworthy when it comes to money. A valuable house, jewelry, large bank account, or other assets can simply be too tempting for someone who puts self above the needs of a helpless and unknowing elder.

Why Can't I Use The Power Of Attorney Document For Medical Decisions?

The Durable Power of Attorney document does not cover healthcare decisions. The permission needed to make someone's healthcare decisions is a different document, sometimes called a "power of attorney for healthcare" or Advance Healthcare Directive. Some states call it a "living will." Whatever it is called where you live, it is specifically for *health care decisions*, and does not deal with money or other business matters. If you have a healthcare power of attorney in some form, it will not permit you to sign checks, sell the house, or close bank accounts. Two separate documents are needed to do good planning for the future: a Durable Power of Attorney (some call it a financial power of attorney) and a Healthcare Directive, or healthcare power of attorney.

Sometimes, members of the U.S. military give a power of attorney document to the spouse at home when they must go off to serve for an extended period of out-of-country military duty. The spouse at home is then able to take out a mortgage on the house, sell property, open or close bank accounts, pay bills, and conduct other financial business without the spouse who also owns the house, property, bank accounts, and so on.

The Durable Power of Attorney document referred to in this chapter is quite similar in regard to what it allows someone to do for an elder. The difference is that a DPOA continues when someone loses capacity to make decisions. The other version of a power of attorney one might have someone use while a person is out of the country is no longer valid when or if the original signer loses the capacity to make financial decisions, as it is not necessarily permanent.

What Is The Difference Between A Power Of Attorney And A Conservatorship/Guardianship?

Either a person appointed by the elder to be power of attorney, or a guardian/conservator is a fiduciary with essentially the same authority to make financial decisions. The most important difference is that a court proceeding is required to appoint a conservator or guardian.

The person who wants the guardianship imposed on an elder can get an attorney. The elder has a right to have an attorney too. The elder who may need a guardian has the right to come to court and present his or her evidence as to why a guardianship is not needed. The elder has the right to fight against a guardianship before the court decides on it. Sometimes the court agrees with the elder who resists having a guardianship. Sometimes it does not. It depends on the kind of evidence lawyers for both sides bring to court.

If a guardian is appointed, the guardian must account regularly to the court about how money is being spent and how much is being spent. The court has the power to oversee what the guardian or conservator does. It can change the guardian, expand or limit the duties involved, and make rulings that affect the power involved. By contrast, the power of attorney does not have to report to a court, and the DPOA document typically does not require that the power of attorney report to anyone about how money is spent. The DPOA is usually permanent.

A guardianship can be temporary, but often becomes permanent after the court learns that the elder needs a permanent guardian after the temporary one reports to the court. It costs less to appoint a durable power of attorney, even if the elder has a lawyer draw up the DPOA document and spend some time going over the matter, and explaining the duties and what it means. Because the court is not involved, it is much simpler for the elder to appoint a DPOA.

What Are The Disadvantages Of Having A Guardianship Or Conservatorship?

The main drawback to using a guardian/conservator rather than a power of attorney is the expense. It costs money to hire a licensed attorney, have the attorney prepare conservatorship/ guardianship papers, file them in court and attend court hearings; as well as follow up on the appointment of the conservator and the formal reporting that the court requires from the conservator.

The attorney goes to court more than once. There is an ongoing requirement to report to the court, usually annually or more often, to account for expenditures. The cost for lawyers, other witnesses, and preparation of the guardianship case will run thousands of dollars when private attorneys are used. The money comes from the elder's assets. All of the steps to the decision by the court are costly and require legal representatives on both sides.

Things said in open court about an elder in front of the elder can be very upsetting and embarrassing to him or her. The procedure should be avoided when possible. However, it may be the only protection available in some cases. It can save an elder from financial ruin, injury, homelessness, and many kinds of self-neglect.

If There Is No Family To Be The Guardian, What Happens?

Family members often serve as guardians/conservators and some do not charge the elder for doing the work. If there is no family member able or willing to be the guardian/conservator, someone outside the family is hired to serve. This kind of guardian is paid by the hour, from the assets of the elder.

A benefit to a conservatorship or guardianship is that the family of the elder, or the elder without family, has some security in knowing that the court is watching what happens to his or her funds and the potential for financial abuse of the elder is at least minimized. Family members can challenge a request for a guardian, which has been presented in court.

The court can appoint a public guardian or other individual willing to serve as a guardian if no family or friend is available. Public guardians work for the county in which the guardianship or conservatorship is filed with the court. They are paid an hourly rate for everything they do, including keeping all financial records, visiting the elder to handle financial matters, and making annual appearances in court to report how money is being spent and the status of the elder.

Using a public guardian to handle the affairs of an elder is not foolproof, but it is far safer than having a questionable person serve as power of attorney with unlimited authority to spend money and sell property. There are instances of financial abuse even by public guardians, but safeguards are built into the system to minimize this risk.

Why Would Someone Need To Hire A Professional Fiduciary?

It makes sense to hire a professional fiduciary if the size of the elder's estate is large, and no one in the family or circle of friends is comfortable or skilled enough to know what to do with the assets. It also makes sense if the person appointed to be power of attorney is not comfortable handling money assets without some objective person to ask when a question comes up. People without adult children who have no reliable relative or friend might appoint a professional fiduciary to be their power of attorney and name that person in the document.

A fiduciary can serve as conservator/guardian, or can be a power of attorney or trustee. A professional fiduciary can serve alongside another person as a co-power of attorney or co-trustee. A professional fiduciary should have certification to be a fiduciary if your state requires certification. A professional fiduciary should also be someone with enough background and experience to make responsible decisions for the elder. Considering that a professional fiduciary is paid by the hour from the elder's money, the hourly rate should be fair in relation to the size of the elder's assets and the fiduciary's credentials and experience.

How Does A Person Find Professional Fiduciaries?

A professional fiduciary could be a retired attorney, accountant, bookkeeper, or other manager. To find one, ask the estate planning attorney who worked with your elder, or who has helped you in the past. Most know qualified fiduciaries. A national fiduciary's organization exists. Their website is at www.nafpa.org. Sometimes the fiduciary is a nurse or care manager.

If you need to hire a professional to handle the money for your aging loved one, be a good consumer. Ask plenty of questions about background, qualifications, state requirements, hourly rates, and experience in this role. Check the background and references. Ask to see the certification. Get all the personal information you would get from an employee on another kind of job.

Be sure you feel comfortable and that the fiduciary prospect gives you a sense of being trustworthy. Ask about how the fiduciary will account for all spending and whether the fiduciary will consult with anyone else about important decisions such as selling property or other assets.

Ten Tips for Handling Money for Aging Loved Ones

1. Get a durable power of attorney document signed and notarized while your aging loved one is competent to understand this important appointment and can make a good decision.

2. Decide together with your aging loved one upon one honest and reliable person to be the power of attorney for finances. Be sure the elder also appoints a backup or successor power of attorney in case the appointed agent gets sick or is unable to serve.

3. Seek legal advice in preparing the Durable Power of Attorney document. For low-income elders, it may be free or at low cost.

4. Bring up the subject of what to do about money in case of incapacity with your aging loved one. If you meet resistance, get help. Do not let it slide, as a crisis can come at any time and everyone needs to be prepared.

5. Watch for warning signs that your elder is slipping or losing the ability to safely handle money. If you see warning signs, act on them. Be prepared to take over the responsibility for finances if you are the power of attorney for finances.

6. Ask questions of your aging parent or loved one about his or her life, social contacts, and involvement with friends and activities. Isolated and lonely seniors are common prey for financial abusers and scam artists.

7. Know where the checkbook is, which bank the elder uses, and what and where the financial resources are. Ask questions and keep records for the time when you may need them.

8. Protect your aging loved one from making money mistakes due to loss of capacity and from financial abuse from scam artists. Take away the checkbook if necessary. A guardianship/ conservatorship is a last resort.

9. Get professional advice if you find it too difficult or you get great resistance in having conversations with your aging loved ones about money.

10. Most of us need help as we age, and that includes help handling money. Face this reality with your aging loved one, and be proactive to prevent a sudden disaster when crisis hits.

References

American Association of Retired Persons (AARP). 601 E Street NW, Washington, DC 20049. http://www.aarp.org.

The National Association of Personal Financial Advisors. http://www.napfa.org.

Chapter Seven
How To Handle Family Conflicts About Elders

Introduction

This chapter of our series digs into an everyday problem that affects most families. Sure, there are lots of families that get along very well. But, there are plenty of families we've encountered who don't get along, and sometimes siblings aren't even speaking to each other. Suddenly, a crisis forces them together to share the tasks of caring for an aging parent, or making decisions about an aging parent. What then?

My experience and that of clinical psychologist, Dr. Mikol Davis, are combined here to offer tips and insights into the problems families face with their aging parents. One of the biggest problems we see is the unrealistic expectation that somehow a sibling who has never taken much responsibility for Mom or Dad in the past will change and begin doing so now, because help is needed. In this chapter, we're trying to help the caregiver sibling see that responsible ones in a family tend to continue to be responsible when caring for aging parents, and irresponsible ones tend to continue to be irresponsible.

Other problems we explore are that of the adult child who is an only child in decision-making, and dealing with conflicting input from various relatives and friends. Our message is to trust yourself, and get competent advice when you feel it is needed. We also address dealing with conflict from the difficult parent.

Caring for aging parents presents a huge challenge for their adult children, especially when those parents suffer with declining health problems over a long period of time. The burden on caregivers is significant. It can bring out the best and worst in a family. We hope that this chapter will help the "responsible one" or ones in the family develop enough perspective of the situation when family is difficult, to get through it. We encourage planning ahead. It can make all the difference.

How to Handle Family Conflicts About Elders

Few family matters are more stressful than those around caring for an aging parent. Those responsible may be in the "sandwich generation," caught between responsibility for their own children, and the responsibility of taking care of their elders. Some have teenagers at home and are dealing with the issues of adolescence while simultaneously managing the changing needs of a declining parent. Others are middle-aged parents of adult children themselves; working and trying to manage the growing needs of their aging loved ones. Others are the only child, responsible for both aging parents.

Some are in conflict with siblings over what to do, making the stress of caregiving even worse. Some families are trying to manage two ill parents at once, and some also have other aging relatives to tend to, besides their own parents. As people reach middle age, disabled siblings may also need care from those who are capable family members. The burden on caregivers can be completely overwhelming.

Many American families are dysfunctional in some way, less than perfect in the way the family members get along. When there has been a history of conflict between or among siblings, or between parent and child, the situation of responsibility forced on the adult child can quickly become a source of extreme stress. In addition, people are living longer with all the care and treatment available for conditions that used to leave us with shorter lives.

Elders with difficult personalities are difficult with health issues on top of their personalities. We have few role models from prior generations who lived as long as our parents may live. We have little to guide us in knowing what to expect. Yet, many family members do take on the care of aging loved ones, willingly and with good intention. As they find themselves in unexpected situations, there is sometimes a feeling of panic, rage, or helplessness.

If the wishes of the elder were never discussed or documented by way of a healthcare directive, or any other document, and the parent loses competency to discuss them, it presents a formidable challenge. Whether you are an only child, or if you have other siblings, the challenge is to try to imagine what your parent would have wanted without being able to ask that parent. Conflicts arise in the decision making about health care and other aspects of aging. The conflicts are not limited to those with siblings.

The Only Child And Conflict Within

The only child has the total burden of caring for Mom or Dad (or other relative) without input from siblings. The benefit is that there is no sibling conflict. However, the burden is that it takes work to figure out what Mom or Dad would have wanted if they could no longer tell you. Investigation by asking other relatives may be an option. Friends of the family, clergy, a parent's attorney, or other resources can provide information to help you form your judgments about what to do.

Sometimes, even when there is no conflict with siblings, there can be conflict with other relatives. An aunt, uncle, or someone who has been close to your parent can cause just as much trouble for you with decision making as a sibling. Even the family physician may disagree with you about whether to resuscitate your parent or to treat an illness when your parent is elderly and frail. Disagreement between two doctors caring for your parent(s) can also be a source of stress.

As an only child, you may be operating in a very emotional state, and in crisis mode. Perhaps your parent has had a stroke, heart attack, or other disabling condition, which leaves you without the opportunity to ask questions of them. A normal reaction to dealing with crisis in a loved one near the end of life, or in advanced years, is to either be in denial or to be completely overwhelmed. Therefore, being able to make rational decisions about the best interests of your parent is even more challenging. In this situation, it can be very helpful to talk to a third person to get a more objective view. A lawyer, clergy person, good friend, your spouse, or other trusted person can assist you in choosing what to do among the alternatives offered to you, sometimes under pressure. If the doctor says, "what do you want to do?" you need to respond.

Once a decision is made to treat or not treat a condition, to resuscitate or not, to move a parent to another living situation, or other serious decision, it is again a normal reaction to have guilt and to second-guess your decision. Guilt and self-doubt will only make the other emotions one is dealing with at the time feel worse. Whether you speak to a counselor, or someone else whom you trust, the help of another person can alleviate some of these conflicting feelings. It can also help you to deal with criticism of your decisions from other family members or friends of your loved one who do not agree with you.

Conflict with others who may not agree with your decisions is better handled if you have taken the time to examine your own feelings and reactions to the decision-making process. The value of consulting with another person, especially if you are an only child, can balance the human tendency to respond primarily from our own fears and issues while making decisions that affect others' lives. It is difficult to be objective about what a parent would want when you are in the middle of a crisis, and are also dealing with your own fears. Now is the time to ask for help. Even if you are independent, willing to help your aging parents and other relatives, and sure you can handle all this, it cannot hurt to run your thoughts by another person and ask for input. This eases the burden you will inevitably feel in making so many caregiver decisions yourself.

If there is no reliable or helpful trusted person in your life, social networks of caregivers are available, and growing. The National Family Caregivers Association, for example, provides support and resources for you, the caregiver, rather than for the aging person for whom you are responsible. Internet chats, message boards, blogs, and other means of connecting through resources like this give you the opportunity to pour out your worries to others who may be in your situation. Local branches of this and similar organizations conduct meetings, retreats, and support groups for caregivers. All of these resources can be helpful for those who are faced with difficult decisions and feel alone in doing so.

Sibling Conflicts

Perhaps you never got along with your sister. Maybe you have had no use for your brother for years. Now, suddenly a crisis forces siblings with old issues between and among them to deal with each other. This is a stress in itself. It can complicate an already stressful situation of an aging parent in failing health who needs the assistance of adult children. What can one do? What should one expect?

It is worth remembering that if a sibling could never be counted on to take responsibility, it is unlikely to change just because a parent is in failing health or has a crisis. Lifelong behavior patterns will still be there, even when it seems that they "should" have changed. In our work, we see many families in which one or more siblings take the lion's share of the burden of caring for aging parents. About 90% of caregivers of aging parents are women.

Without speculating as to all the reasons why this may be so, we can look at the statistics and conclude that if you are the daughter, there is a pretty good chance that you will be the responsible one caring for an aging parent. Some sons are excellent caregivers and fully devoted to the task, and we see this in our practice also. Whether you are a son or a daughter of an aging parent, if you have siblings, the primary caregiver sibling may feel that the burden of managing the parent's care falls unfairly on him or her.

Sometimes sibling conflicts are a result of geography: one adult child lives near the aging parent. The other(s) live out of the area. The adult child nearby is somewhat required to take care of things, simply because she is close by. This can lead to resentment on the part of the one who must "do it all." Even for those who willingly take on the many tasks of managing the care of an aging parent until the end of life, it is inevitable that caregivers will feel the burden. Depression is quite common among adult children who take care of their parents. The job is demanding and stressful. Physical and mental decline in a parent can cause enormous emotional upheaval in the adult child, who watches the parent's strength, vitality and mental faculties ebb away.

Although the work of caregiver can have many noble, beautiful and even humorous moments, it is also filled with hard physical effort and emotional turmoil. It can lead to angry exchanges between the direct or primary caregiver and the sibling or siblings who are not as involved. In these instances, old conflicts between siblings, which have been dormant for years, can boil to the surface. Nasty, bitter exchanges of words, telephone calls or emails can come from the bed of resentment which could well have remained dormant were it not for the state of Mom's or Dad's health. If you are in this situation with your siblings, what can you do?

The underlying dynamic of these conflicts is often found in expectations. The expectation may sound like this: if our parent needs a lot of care and attention, everyone should step up and share the load. Though this may, indeed, be a reasonable expectation, it may not be a realistic one. Family members who have historically been responsible will likely continue to be so at the last phase of a parent's life. Those who have not been comfortable with or at least willing to take responsibility for a parent are unlikely to do so at the last phase. Resentment can be mitigated by changing one's expectations.

It can be very difficult to accept the fact that one person or two in a group of siblings is doing all the work. It is unfair. It can stay that way for a long time, even for years. However, there is no changing a sibling's character. The primary caregiver(s) can and should ask the available and able siblings to share the work. Stating one's needs and expectations clearly and in a non-threatening way is a good start.

For example, one can say to a sibling, "I'm taking Mom to the doctor twice this week, besides making sure she gets all her medicines every day. Will you help me out by taking her to her appointments next week?"

A direct approach does not work for everyone. Different styles work for different people. The point, though, is to ask for what one needs, rather than expect that another sibling will simply step in and help because it should be obvious that help is needed. In many families, it just doesn't work that way. For those in the primary caregiver role, failing to ask for help, and silently fuming about not getting help can only lead to angry outbursts, and possibly to depression and resentment. Even when you ask for help, one must be prepared for the possibility that one will not get it. Middle-aged siblings may have a million excuses for not helping you.

A way to manage your own mental health is to be prepared for not having help from siblings, and to alter your expectations of help if it is not forthcoming. If you can afford to pay for assistance, don't hesitate to get it. We all need all the support and assistance with the chores that we can get in our caring for aging parents. If funds are limited, you have no choice but to forge ahead and do the work yourself, even as your sibling or siblings seem to stand by and "do nothing." In that case, enlist the help of friends, churches or synagogues, community agencies, volunteers, and whatever resources you can locate in your area. There is no need to be a martyr and take on the burden alone, while resenting deeply that the weight all falls on you.

For those who are not in the habit of asking for help from others, remember that this is a special exception to what your life was like before. Your parents or other aging relatives will only go down this road once. Without help, you can end up sick yourself, depressed, or unable to help. If you cannot rely on siblings, rely on others who are more willing. Once you reach out, you may be surprised and gratified to learn that many people are kind, generous and willing to give some time to you and your loved one to make things a little easier. Asking for help from others will do much to alleviate the risk of rage, resentment, and physical upset over siblings who have let you down. Should your parent resist or complain about "outsiders" coming in to help, it must be pointed out that the help you have solicited is for *you,* and that you are doing the best you can.

Controlling Conflict Through Finding The Leader

It is important in a family to quickly identify one sibling who is going to take the leadership role. If you have difficulty identifying who will take that role, then it is necessary to select a leader by volunteering, by rotation, or by election from the others. The person identified must be willing. The next step is to identify the extent of the needs of the aging loved one. This identification may be very difficult if you are a distance caregiver. Even if you live in the same community as the aging parent, it can still be difficult to identify the extent of a parent's needs. We find that this is a daunting job for many families, due to the fact that one's own ideas and beliefs about aging color the process.

One's personal fears, beliefs about how things should be and denial of the parent's decline in health and ability can distort the process of identification of a parent's needs. In our practice, we see adult children volunteering for the care of aging parents with a naïve view of the extent of a parent's true level of need. The vision, in the adult child's mind, of what will be involved, turns out to be far less than what actually is needed on a daily basis. Therefore, it is in the best interest of the distant caregivers to take advantage of the assistance of a geriatric care manager to help get a realistic assessment. (See the "How to Find and Use a Care Manager" chapter.)

A professional assessment can give everyone a neutral basis for decision-making. It beats arguing about the level of function Mom or Dad is capable of performing. It can also help the parent, who must be a part of the conversation for as long as the parent is capable of participating. When the parent's needs have been identified, it is up to the leader of the siblings or other family members to initiate the services and care necessary to meet those needs.

For those who cannot afford to hire a care manager, the leader can seek a needs assessment from the local social services department of your county, or from other senior services organizations in your area. Social workers, public health nurses, or other geriatric care workers can be very helpful in sorting out what your parent needs in a neutral and objective way, which can, in turn, eliminate sibling fighting about what is best. Your area Agency on Aging is a helpful resource.

Once a professional assessment has been completed, a plan is usually suggested. The social worker, nurse, or professional geriatric care manager is familiar with the resources in the community and can offer alternatives and help with connecting the aging parent to those resources. It will also do much to avert sibling conflicts about what a parent needs, the costs associated with care, and the alternatives available to meet the parent's needs in the community. This gives the entire family a roadmap to plan for the parent's present needs, and a projection of future needs as well. A roadmap, which will probably be called a care plan, will give the family members involved with it a basis to divide the labor and share the responsibility if they are willing.

Avoiding Conflict Through Advance Planning

This chapter makes a point of urging everyone to talk with your elders while they still have the ability to make decisions and tell you what they want toward the end of life. Preventive care, in the form of good, frank talk about what the future may hold, can do much to avoid the family hassle. Prevention of conflict can arise from written documents such as a "living will" or advance healthcare directive. At least we know what the elder wants concerning the end of life if we have had them write it down on this document. The benefit of such a document, which everyone should have, is twofold. First, it lets every family member know what to do if the time comes that your loved one is unable to speak or make decisions. Second, it serves as a guide to the family, even if the family may be in disagreement. This is what Dad wanted. Dad's wishes should be honored.

An example of how the healthcare directive could prevent family conflict is found in the situation when the elder has signed this document and stated in it that she did not want any extraordinary measures taken to prolong her life. If she later has a cardiac arrest (heart attack) and is in a coma, the doctors should honor her desire not to be resuscitated if she stops breathing. Even if an adult child wants "everything done," the child's wishes matter less than the elder's wishes. The doctor has the assurance that if the elder is not resuscitated; the doctor is doing what his patient wants.

What if there are two siblings, and one wants Mom resuscitated and the other is arguing with her that Mom did not want that? What if the sibling who wants resuscitation refuses to recognize the "no extraordinary measures" directive and tells the doctor to resuscitate Mom if she stops breathing? What can one do?

If siblings are in conflict over a parent's care and they are unable to work it out between or among them, it may be time to get help. Using a neutral person to assist can do a great deal to bring objectivity to the fight. Mediation is using a neutral person to help both sides in a conflict work out their own solution. The mediator provides guidance, information, and feedback. A mediator can guide a discussion to resolution if the parties are willing to resolve the matter. As a mediator myself, I am a strong advocate for using this method to reduce disputes or find solutions. It is effective in all situations, regardless of the subject, approximately 80% of the time. That success rate seems much better than the success rate of siblings at war trying to work out a conflict without help.

How Does Mediation Work?

Typically, when a situation has reached the point that it does not seem feasible that the people involved can keep a conflict in control, and emotions are high, they have to think about getting someone outside the conflict to help them. Let's say there are four family members in disagreement. Two are on one side of a question and two are on the other side. All four would have to agree to sit down with a neutral person for the purpose of trying to work out their differences, as a first step.

The next step is finding a mediator. There are community mediation services all over the U.S., particularly in larger cities. Courts frequently use mediators to try to settle cases, which are filed, in court, in hopes of averting trial. Most court cases, which go to mediation, get settled in mediation. Courts have lists of local attorneys and other mediators trained in resolving disputes, available to help. Private mediators usually charge a fee for their services. In using a private mediator, you may be able to get a neutral person who is familiar with the issues you are facing in your family. You will pay a fee by the hour or by the mediation, but you are most likely to get a mediator whose credentials match your problem.

For example, if the dispute involves an elder, you would look for someone who does elder mediation, and has training or a background providing some expertise in this area. If the dispute were about a parent's estate, you would look for someone who has experience in probate law, real estate, family conflicts, or related matters. The mediator's experience level is important.

Volunteer mediators often staff community mediation centers. They are likely to be low cost or no cost for low-income clients. You may get lucky and find one who has the skill or background you are looking for, or you may not. However, a highly skilled mediator may be able to resolve most kinds of conflict, even if he or she does not have exactly the background that matches your problem. Finding a good mediator is a matter of the consumer trusting the person to be neutral and show leadership in keeping the parties on track in trying to get their problem solved. If the trust is not there, it will be difficult to accept suggestions or information from a mediator.

People who want to try to resolve a problem at mediation are usually most comfortable with someone who understands the kind of issue they are presenting and has a background related to the subject at hand. As an example, if someone is involved in a dispute about ownership of a piece of property, it may be very helpful to have a mediator who is well versed in property law.

Mediators vary in personality and style as much as people in general vary in this regard. A good consumer who has the means to pay for a private mediator should research the proposed mediator, check out any website the mediator has which would highlight his or her background, and ask for a summary of the mediator's experience.

Many mediators are attorneys, though mediation does not require a law degree or any license. It does require training and experience. If you are a consumer who is paying for a mediator, find the best person you can for the price charged. Search the Internet, check local directory listings, and ask an attorney if you know one, who can refer you to a qualified mediator. A website, www.Mediate.com, has listings across the U.S. However, local mediators may also advertise locally.

Does The Mediator Decide How The Dispute Should Turn Out?

No, the mediator does not make any decisions for the people who are involved in a conflict. The mediator is not the judge of who is right and who is wrong. Rather, the mediator can be like a referee, a go-between, or a person who draws out what people really want in the course of talking about a problem. A mediator is not in a position, legally or otherwise, to make a ruling on anything, nor to tell anyone what to do. A skilled mediator can do a great deal to help people find their own way out of a problem by encouraging them and helping them to reach their own solutions, compromises, and agreements.

What Is The Difference Between Mediation And Arbitration?

There is a great deal of difference between mediation and arbitration. Arbitration is a formal process in which a dispute is decided, often in a final way. Arbitration may take the place of a trial in court. It may have lawyers representing each side. The arbitrator is in position to judge who is right and who is wrong.

The arbitrator does make a ruling or decision. Arbitration may come about as a result of a contract a person signed. For example, if one has a dispute with an employer, the worker might be required to go to arbitration instead of trial at the end of a legal case. In those situations, the ruling or decision of the arbitrator is final, and the losing party has to do what the arbitrator ruled, or accept the result of arbitration, depending on what kind of decision is made.

On the other hand, mediation is a less formal process. If a lawsuit is involved, attorneys will attend the mediation in hopes of getting the case settled. If a lawsuit is not filed, there may not be any lawyers at all. In elder mediations, there might not be any lawyers, as these can involve family member in conflict with family member, and there is no legal case. The dispute can be with siblings, adult child or children and parent(s), and with caregivers and residents in care facilities. Mediation can be very helpful in reducing the anger and fear that often accompany issues with elders in failing health.

Sometimes, lawsuits are filed and siblings have hired attorneys to fight each other. In those instances, the lawyers can assist in encouraging their clients to work with the mediator, to speak openly about their needs and wants, and to work on possible solutions. However, there are times we find that attorneys representing family members at family mediations do more harm than good. They are vigorously advocating for their clients, but do little to help work things out.

The disadvantage of using attorneys at private family mediations is the cost. The participants at mediation are paying their attorneys by the hour, and paying the mediator by the hour. It gets quite expensive. When a matter is pending in court, however, using attorneys at mediation is far less expensive than paying them to take a case to trial. Ideally, a skilled attorney advocate will counsel the client to use the mediation process to work out a settlement of the problem at hand, using the mediator's help and input. Attorneys with their clients' best interests in mind encourage the use of mediation as a useful and most often successful means of settling a pending dispute.

Parent-Adult Child Conflicts

Adult children who find that parents are in need of help may find themselves in conflict with their parents over the idea that any help is needed. The conflict may have many causes. Elders of baby boomer children are survivors of the Depression. They are socialized to "tough it out," "keep a stiff upper lip," and to try to avoid burdening anyone else. Elders who grew up during this era have likely never discussed their own feelings much, or at all. They may be very polite and uncomfortable around confrontation, and even more uncomfortable around conflict. They may not actually have the vocabulary to discuss their emotions in any detail. "I'm fine" and "we'll be fine" may be as far as it goes.

The culture of being independent and the ingrained habits of not asking for help can truly be a source of conflict with their children when Mom and Dad begin to lose the ability to care for themselves.

Again, as discussed at more length in the "How to Manage a Dangerous Older Driver" chapter, the fear of loss of control often motivates the refusal of help. Parents simply do not want to face the possibility of dependency, being "put in a home," having to give up their right to decide everything for themselves, or any other thing which is seen as a threat. When well meaning adult children approach parents with the prospect of getting help or giving help, strong resistance can cause tremendous stress for the adult children.

There may be an intense level of unspoken fear from the parents about loss of control of their finances, their physical health, and their ability to live independently. Planning in advance and having the necessary, though difficult, conversations we have discussed throughout this book can do much to reduce conflict. The advance planning conversations lay a foundation for further discussion when the time comes to implement the parents' wishes. Lack of advance planning with parents who do not like to face the possibility of needing anyone to help them is likely to breed conflict when adult children bring up the subject later. When there is no advance planning, conflict is further worsened because siblings may disagree about what to say, what to do, and what is good for their parent.

Where Do I Start?

If there has been no advance planning, where do you start? If you live in your parents' area, and you have noticed a significant decline in their abilities over time, you are at an advantage. At least you have more frequent contact and a basis for having a conversation with them than those adult children who live at a distance have. If the information your parent gives you about not needing help comes only from talking to them on the telephone, you cannot truly know the extent of any problems they may have. Start by making a visit. If it is inconvenient, consider that it will probably be much more inconvenient to get a call in the middle of the night advising you that Mom or Dad is in the hospital, and you have no idea what to do, once you get there.

Think of your advance-planning visit as a preventive step to take for yourself. You will manage any crisis that comes up down the road far better if you know who the doctors are, where the financial documents are kept, what medications your parents take, what kinds of insurance they have, and where the policies are kept. There are many guidelines and checklists available on the internet to assist you in doing advance planning with your parents. Starting the conversation about these matters is up to you if your parents do not do so. When is the right time? Some people advocate the "40-70" rule. That is, if you are in your 40s or older, and your parents are 70 years old or older, it's time.

Talking about factual information on such subjects as where the mortgage is held (if there is one), where the bank accounts are located, what the doctor's name and address is, and the like are good ways to start the process. It is often easier to discuss facts first, and then to transition to the more emotional subjects such as what kind of care one wants or can afford if one becomes frail or sick. If your parent avoids going into these subjects, it is up to you to press them do so, however gently.

Without the necessary information that planning in advance will yield, your family is a time bomb for conflict. Avoiding conflict is possible, but it takes effort. Someone must always take the initiative to have the difficult conversation.

These planning conversations are not always the worst things you could imagine. Some elders have already experienced losses of siblings, friends, or spouses. They may be more ready to discuss these things than you think, because they are living the aging process, while you are observing them. The advantage of a visit to your parent for the purpose of having this conversation can be that you will have time to revisit any subject your parent resists.

If for example, you say, "Dad, we really need to talk about finances now," and your father refuses, you can say that you need to talk about it tomorrow, and you will still be there the next day. You need to bring it up repeatedly on such a visit. In overcoming a parent's resistance to talking about these emotionally laden matters, it is important to dispel the myth that not discussing it will be less burdensome on you, the adult child. You will need to point out, respectfully, that it will be much worse of a burden on you if the subject is not talked about, because you have no way of knowing how to help your parent in a crisis if the subject is not discussed.

On your advance-planning visit to your parent, we encourage you to make notes, or use a tape or digital recorder. Once you have recorded what your parent wants to say, you have a tool available to you that can prevent or reduce conflict in the future. Your parent may later experience memory loss, which is increasingly problematic, as people grow older. The risk of dementia, and particularly Alzheimer's disease, rises with age. If your parent forgets, you have their own words to remind you and the parent, of what they wanted and what was said at a clearer time. The recording of this information can also reduce the risk of sibling conflicts over what Mom or Dad really did want before she or he lost the ability to recall this information.

The Stonewalling Parent

Some parents cannot be convinced by gentle persuasion to discuss subjects such as finances, their health, or other matters they consider no one else's business. In those situations, it is again time to seek help. The consequences of not doing any advance planning and refusing to let the adult children know where to find the necessary documents and information can be disastrous.

Enormous expenses for attorneys and court proceedings can come from parents' refusal to disclose things a caregiver must know at the time of an emergency. If your parent is willing to let you come along to a doctor visit, that may be a way to get information from the doctor as to what is needed, and what medicines your parent requires. If your parent has a lawyer, financial planner, accountant, bookkeeper, stockbroker, clergy person, or other trusted person, it may be easier for your parent to allow you to speak with that individual than for your loved one to talk directly to you. Ask for permission. If your parent does not, for some reason, trust you or your judgment, seek the help of someone the parent does trust. Perhaps there is another relative, a good friend, the parent's sibling, or someone your loved one respects. Ask for help with this difficult situation.

Someone who is not emotionally involved is more likely to appreciate the urgent need to get the information for advance planning. The advance planning information is what is important. Who, in particular, obtains it is less important. If the trusted person can make a good record for you, you are ahead of the game in trying to avert the conflicts that come from assumptions and confusion later on.

Finally, it is good to know that so many resources are available to baby boomers and their parents for the planning process. What to talk about in the difficult conversation is listed for you in some of these resources. Checklists of the necessary information everyone needs are available through attorneys, legal aid offices, senior centers, Agency on Aging offices, social services, books, and on the Internet.

We recommend a very complete resource in DVD format, Aging Parents, available on our website at www.AgingParents.com. Using these tools can help you head off conflict before it starts.

Seven Tips For Dealing With Family Conflicts About Elders

---

1. For only children of aging parents; if you become confused about making decisions for an incompetent parent, seek the advice of a trusted other person.

2. If you have a sibling who has never shared the workload, don't expect the sibling to change because your parent's need is greater than ever.

3. Reduce your own stress by changing your expectations of others.

4. To avert conflict over what the parent needs, get a needs assessment done by an objective professional.

5. Plan ahead before crisis hits. Have the difficult conversation with your elders sooner, not later.

6. Remember the 40-70 Rule: if you're in your 40s and your parent is in his 70s or older, it's time to talk about possible incapacity in the future.

7. If you need outside help for family conflicts that are spinning out of control, consider using a professional mediator. A neutral person can help families make agreements.

References

Mediate Resolution Services. PO Box 51090. Eugene, Oregon 97405. (541) 345-1629. http://www.mediate.com.

Carter, Elizabeth and Monica McGoldrick. 1980. *The Family Life Cycle, A Framework For Family Therapy*. New York: Gardner Press.

Chapter Eight
How to Find a Good Lawyer for Mom or Dad

Introduction

This chapter touches on a subject near, but not always dear to my heart: the way lawyers treat clients. The adult child who thinks Mom or Dad needs to update the estate plan, or get a durable power of attorney document done, is correct. All of these things need to be done for our parents. If your aging parent has not updated any documents, or doesn't have any, it is time to act.

Choosing a lawyer can be difficult if you don't know someone in the elder law field. It is always best to get a personal recommendation from someone who has experience with an elder law attorney in your area. Even that, however, is no guarantee that your parent will be treated well, or that the attorney will do good quality work.

This chapter is intended to help your parent to be a good consumer of legal services. If your aging parents have never done any estate planning or have never thought about what will happen to their property and money after they're gone, the adult child can urge a parent to get to it and see a lawyer. The adult child can help the parent find a lawyer, but it is the parent, not the adult child, who is the client. In choosing a lawyer, there are things to watch out for, warning signs that perhaps the one you just talked to isn't for you, and that you should keep looking.

It can be very frustrating to go about the process of choosing a lawyer. They may not call back, they may seem to be in a hurry, and other things can make the process daunting. The tips we offer here can help you bypass the lawyers who are not a good fit for your aging parent. When it comes to finding a lawyer, we hope that you will use the information here to be wise about your choices.

Protecting aging parents from a poor choice of lawyers is, as I see it, part of the role of the caring adult child; as long as your parent will permit you to help. Because your parent is the client, and you are not, it is always the parent's choice that must come first. However, when there is trust between parent and adult child, your input can be a fine source of guidance to get your parent to someone who will do a good job legally and personally.

How to Find a Good Lawyer for Mom or Dad

Most people seem to be somewhat uncomfortable with the idea of seeing a lawyer. First, the task of finding one you like can seem daunting. But even if you find a lawyer you like, it can be difficult to determine whether the lawyer is actually doing a good job. The average person has little to go on by way of comparison of a lawyer's work against any sort of standard. After all, one cannot go around looking at other people's wills or trusts to see if they stack up against the will or trust your lawyer is drawing up for your aging loved one. So, how does one begin to look for a qualified lawyer?

Communication

Unfortunately, law schools do not teach communication skills as a part of the standard curriculum. One does not need to be good at "people skills" to pass the state bar examination. A qualified lawyer can be very good at the technical aspects of legal work and terrible at relating to people. By way of analogy, some physicians are really great technically, but have no "bedside manner." Having practiced as a lawyer for the past thirty years and dealing with hundreds of individuals, my perspective is that the client deserves certain basics if he/she is willing to pay an attorney for time, work, or legal representation.

One essential is that the prospective client deserves a chance to briefly meet with or at least talk to the attorney, without being charged for the attorney's time, to simply see if it feels like a good fit. There is no law, which grants any consumer this right. Rather, it is simply a courtesy. My perspective, which may not be shared by lawyer colleagues everywhere, is that if someone who doesn't know me is willing to trust me enough to pay for my time, that person has a right to meet me and ask questions before writing a check.

So, I recommend that you contact the lawyer you are considering asking for assistance, and interview the lawyer briefly. If you like the tone and type of answers you get, go forward. If you are put off by an abrupt manner, the lawyer seems to be in a hurry, or you are not comfortable with anything about the lawyer, keep looking.

Law schools do not typically teach communication skills, and many people have never learned these skills in a formal way, or at all. Many lawyers do not have good communication skills. An example of a communication skill is what is called "active listening." This is the ability to sit still, make eye contact, and focus attention on the person talking (the prospective client) without interrupting, unless the client gets off track. Active listening also means asking appropriate questions based on what the client has just said. If the lawyer constantly interrupts you, does not seem to hear what you are saying, is checking email while you are speaking, or otherwise does not seem to be paying attention, this is a clue to how the lawyer does business. Look for a lawyer with the basics: good listening skills, the ability to communicate respect for your loved one and that person's problem, and the ability to inspire confidence in the lawyer's legal skills.

The ability to listen without interrupting someone's sentence is surprisingly uncommon. If your loved one's prospective lawyer does not have this ability, it is a good idea to interview someone else. You will certainly need to tell the lawyer what you want before she/he can begin the job. If the lawyer makes it difficult for you to get your point across, it is a bad sign and you can do better.

This is not the same as the lawyer redirecting you to the question he or she has asked you. Many of us wander from the point, lose track of the question, or have a "senior moment" and forget what we wanted to say. A good lawyer with good communication skills will politely redirect your response to the question or information the lawyer is trying to get. You will know that he or she is doing this well if you do not feel uncomfortable or offended by this polite kind of "interruption."

A good lawyer will respect that you are the one paying for legal service, and help you by providing the necessary data to go forward with the work, rather than allowing you to ramble on endlessly, in a way that does not help the lawyer go forward with the work. The lawyer is supposed to know what is necessary to get the job done, and what data is needed from you or your elder loved one. At the hourly rates lawyers charge, it is not a social visit or time for an undirected chat, though your aging parent may forget that. It is a good indicator if the lawyer is able to keep the flow of information coming, focusing throughout the appointment on what the lawyer needs to get in order to serve the client.

Another "must," which can be missed, is the common courtesy of responding to your telephone calls. When I graduated from law school, I attended a workshop with a panel of speakers, on starting one's own law practice. It was very informative. One of the things I learned was that the most common consumer complaint against attorneys is the failure to return telephone calls. I was a bit shocked. This seemed to suggest that lawyers are rude. How disillusioning to hear this about my newly embraced profession. I quickly learned that the advice was well given. As a newly practicing lawyer working in a firm, many lawyers I called in the usual course of business did not return my calls. I had to become very persistent to get what I wanted.

How much worse it must have been for consumers, who may have felt intimidated or shy to keep pestering a lawyer who failed to return a telephone call. Consumers may assume that lawyers are busy, and this is often the case. However, common courtesy can be had, even with a busy lawyer. If the lawyer repeatedly fails to return your calls, find one with better manners. Alternatively, email is a way of avoiding telephone tag. It is a good idea at the first interview to find out if the lawyer you are considering will communicate with you by email or with your loved one (if Mom or Dad uses email), what the charge is for doing so, and if getting emails from a client is an option the lawyer accepts.

It is your right as a consumer of legal services for which you are paying to receive a reasonably prompt response when you contact an attorney who is giving legal services to you. If you do not use email, or you prefer letters or telephone calls, beware of lawyers who do not respond to your written requests for information or an update on your matter within a reasonable time. A day or two to get back to you by telephone, and a week or so to answer a letter seems fair. Longer than that may be a danger sign that this lawyer has a problem with time management, is overloaded with work, or does not have adequate office assistance to keep you informed.

As you cannot easily compare the attorney's work with work he or she has done for other clients in the same way you can compare the tangible services of say, one gardener with another gardener, what can you use to figure out how to find out who is a good lawyer?

As with many professional services, personal recommendations can be very useful. They are, however, not foolproof. Lawyers often specialize. If you want to get a trust prepared and find an attorney who is wonderful at construction litigation, but does not prepare trusts, that is not the right attorney for your aging loved ones. Your neighbor's best friend's cousin, though known to your neighbor, is not necessarily a good lawyer for your parent.

So, ask good questions about the lawyer someone recommends to you. What kind of lawyer is she/he? Do you know if this recommended lawyer has solid experience in the field of estate planning, or your matter? It takes more than a lawyer who is a nice person to do a good job.

Do You Need A Specialist?

In some fields of law, attorneys can become "certified specialists." This means that the state bar in a particular state has defined how much experience and testing are required to have this designation. In California, one can become a "certified specialist" in estate planning. The State Bar of California's standards for attorney certification in estate planning, trust and probate law can be found at www.CalBar.org. These may be similar in other states.

The amount of experience and extra testing the lawyer has gone through to have this designation is a good sign, but not a guarantee, that the lawyer is going to do a good job for you or your loved one. You must still be a good consumer and interview the lawyer to see if your loved one "clicks" with the lawyer, as well as checking out some references, and asking good questions of the lawyer you are considering.

For example, you might ask: How many trusts/wills have you prepared? How often do you have your clients update the estate plan you prepare for them? Are you a member of any professional organizations in this field? Ask questions which pertain to your family's situation. Check with the State Bar where you live to find out if the lawyer is a "certified specialist" or if your state provides certification in the specialty area you are seeking. A helpful website is managed by the National Academy of Elder Law Attorneys, and is located at www.naela.org.

Attorneys who operate in a professional manner always tell you what the charge is, by hourly or flat rate, for the service you want. They are required by the State Bar to provide you with a written fee agreement, which spells out the fee arrangement, unless the amount of work done is very small. In California, the State Bar requires a written fee agreement for any amounts to be charged to a client if the fees are over $1000.00. Your signature is needed to enter into the arrangement.

Many lawyers also send an "engagement letter," shortly after the first meeting, which reiterates the agreement for legal services contemplated and states the fee agreement. This is good practice, and is a sign of a professional way of doing business. Again, such letters and fee agreements are not necessary if the lawyer meets with you for perhaps an hour, gives you information and advice, and does no other work.

If you are trying to get your parent to an estate-planning lawyer, plan ahead. Does your family have conflicts already over your parent's money? Do you have unreasonable or contentious siblings or other potential heirs to the parent's estate? Do you think that no matter what your parent does to create or change an estate plan, someone will fight the distribution of money or property after your parent passes away? If you are concerned that a fight over your parent's estate is going to happen, encourage your parent to find an attorney who does "probate litigation" as well as estate planning.

This is another specialized area of law, and not every estate-planning attorney is willing or inclined to do litigation. It takes a certain type of personality to succeed in the field of litigation, and not every lawyer is suited for it. In fact, most lawyers do not do litigation.

Some attorneys are capable and experienced both at drafting the necessary documents such as trusts and wills, to have a proper estate plan in place, and at defending the estate plan from legal attack by a dissatisfied heir later on. In seeking out an attorney to help you with adequate estate planning, look at the family situation in making your decision about which lawyer is right for the job.

Know Whom The Lawyer Represents

One important ethical point to keep in mind is that a lawyer has an obligation to the person or persons she or he represents, and not to the client's family members. If, for example, you come with your aging parent to meet with a lawyer, and you are a potential heir of your parent, the lawyer cannot represent both of you at the same time. If your parent has given you a Durable Power of Attorney concerning finances the lawyer may choose to talk to both you and your aging parent at the same time. Under that circumstance, the lawyer must ask your parent for permission to speak about the matter at hand in front of you. Your parent can also give permission for you to be present for any conversation with the attorney, but the lawyer must ask and be sure this is correct.

Otherwise, client confidentiality requires that the lawyer excuse the family member(s) from the room and talk confidentially with the client alone. This may be a confusing point for some adult children who are trying to get their parents to plan ahead and get their trust set up, or the will updated. Adult children may just be trying to help.

In some instances, the help comes with a -interest: if the estate plan is done properly, the adult child will likely inherit money, if any money is available to inherit. The lawyer is in a clear ethical position to represent only the elder. If you are the adult child, do not expect the lawyer to advise you, personally, if she or he represents your mother or father, unless you are the current power of attorney for your mother or father.

This prevents a conflict of interest for the lawyer. Client confidentiality is a serious consideration for any attorney and is required by every state bar. If the lawyer represents a competent elder, the lawyer does not have to tell the adult child or children what the elder wants to do with his or her money or property.

For the lawyer to represent both adult child and parent, informed consent of the parent is required. "Informed consent" means that the lawyer has given information to the elder about his or her rights to keep the estate information confidential, and the parent has given permission for the lawyer to reveal the information, based on being fully aware of what he or she is giving up in terms of confidentiality.

Finding A Lawyer For Elder Neglect Or Elder Abuse Cases

If your matter involves questions of elder neglect, abuse, or medical negligence issues, and these are what bring you to an attorney, be sure to ask questions as to how many cases of this kind the lawyer has handled. In this area of the law also, some lawyers prefer the "rough and tumble" of litigation, while others avoid it. Cases involving neglect or negligence all have the potential to end up in litigation, which means that they might have to be filed in court, and go through the long legal process following filing a case with the court.

This is a very specialized area. It requires a specialized person to handle such a matter. Do not be misled into thinking that the attorney who never does litigation of this kind (or at all) can just "write a letter" and things will be fine. A negligence claim is a most serious situation, which must be handled competently from the very beginning. In matters, which come from medical or institutional negligent care of the aging parent, the lawyer may represent all family members, only if all are damaged by the negligent acts alleged in the case.

The first contact an attorney makes with an opposing party, in representing your aging parent, can have considerable influence in how your matter turns out. If you are seeking legal help for your elder loved one who is unable to seek this help on his own, seek a lawyer who seems to have an interest in your loved one's plight. Again, this is a feeling that you get at the time of your contact with the lawyer. First impressions do count. If you have an uneasy feeling talking to the lawyer, if you feel talked down to, or if the lawyer just seems unapproachable, try someone else. In many urban areas, there is certainly no shortage of lawyers. The most highly qualified, likable lawyers, however, may not be plentiful.

Has The Lawyer Ever Been Disciplined By The Bar?

A wise consumer will check the attorney's state bar record, while considering whether to hire a particular attorney. The state bar is the governmental organization which issues the licenses for attorneys to practice law in your state, and disciplines those who act in violation of state bar standards. The state bar of your state likely has a public record of discipline of attorneys.

For example, there is a public record of any disciplinary action against attorneys listed on the California State Bar website, www.calbar.org. Although it is quite rare for someone who is unlicensed to pose as an attorney, it has happened. The website will give you the address of the attorney and the attorney's state bar number. Check to see if the address is current and matches the one where you plan to see the attorney. If the attorney has moved and not updated his or her business address, the attorney is already in violation of a state bar requirement. The licensed attorney's business address listing is a public record, available to anyone.

You can log on to the state bar website to see if any record of discipline for a particular attorney exists. Complaints by consumers are not listed as discipline unless the bar has investigated, filed an action against the attorney, and an outcome has occurred. Pending matters against attorneys are not listed on the public record until finalized. The record of discipline will include any punishment such as probation, fines, or suspension of the attorney's license to practice law. If discipline or suspension has ever occurred, it is prudent to choose a different lawyer with a clean record.

Seven Tips for Finding a Good Lawyer

---

1. Use personal recommendations from friends, but ask questions. Is this lawyer a good fit for you and your problem? Do the work to investigate.

2. Interview the lawyer before you sign up with the lawyer. See if the meeting feels comfortable.

3. Get a reference and find out about the lawyer's past experience with your particular problem. Even if the lawyer has helped you before on another matter, he or she may not have skill in the area where you need it. For estate planning, go to an estate planning lawyer. For litigation, go to an attorney who does litigation on a daily basis.

4. For estate planning attorneys, consider whether a Certified Specialist will suit your needs better than an attorney who is not certified. Certification applies only to some legal areas, and is no guarantee of a good lawyer. Likewise, lack of certification is not necessarily a sign of lack of skill or legal competence in estate planning, or anything else.

5. Check the attorney's state bar record. Look for any past discipline and check for a current address.

6. Expect the attorney to be courteous and to return your telephone calls within a day or two. Beware of attorneys who do not return calls.

7. Trust your instincts. If it doesn't "feel right" with a lawyer you interview, find someone else.

In summary, finding a lawyer to do proper planning for you takes work. Making a negligence claim on behalf of your elder loved one who may have been injured or neglected is a serious consideration. Take the time to look thoroughly if you need a lawyer. The careful consumer will go to the trouble to be sure the lawyer is qualified, courteous, and professional.

References

American Association of Retired Persons (AARP). 601 E Street NW, Washington, DC 20049. http://www.aarp.org.

National Academy of Elder Law Attorneys Inc. 1604 North Country Club Road, Tucson, AZ 85716. http://www.naela.org.

"Standards for Attorney Certification in Estate Planning, Trust and Probate Law," State Bar of California. San Francisco (Main Office), 180 Howard Street, San Francisco, CA 94105. http://calbar.ca.gov/calbar/pdfs/rules/Rules_Title3_Div2-Ch4_LegSpec_Estate.pdf

Chapter Nine
How to Stand Up for Your Elder in the Health Care System

Introduction

Few systems in our society are as complex as the health care system. The number of services, the breadth of their reach, and the time it takes to understand them can overwhelm the adult children of aging parents. The sheer complexity of the system lends itself to errors, duplication, lost files, and poor communication. It can also lend itself to deadly errors in care.

This chapter is a guide to help the boomer with an aging parent receiving health care to learn when and how to speak up when something goes wrong. This may sound intimidating. Usually, we hesitate. Maybe we're wrong. They're all so busy. Maybe it will get better. There seems to be a normal and natural resistance to doing things in the health care system, which seem like rocking the boat.

However, if you do not stand up for your parent or loved one, costly mistakes can occur. Speaking up for your parent is not a duty anyone told you about in school. Chances are, most people did not have to speak up for a parent until the parent became ill or frail and really needed help. But as our aging parents live on, and have more things that seem to get in the way of their own ability to stand up for themselves, there is not much choice about this.

As an experienced advocate for individuals for my entire legal career, I have developed the skill set a lawyer needs to be assertive on behalf of a client. I recognize that speaking up and being an advocate does not come naturally for most of us. However, it is my hope that with a little encouragement that you will find in this chapter, and a little guidance in finding your way through the system, you can stick up for a vulnerable aging parent when your help is needed.

What do I mean by sticking up for an aging parent? I mean not letting a health insurer deny a claim the insurer is supposed to pay without raising a fuss. I mean questioning billing that doesn't look right. I mean asking the right questions when your loved one is not getting the care he or she is supposed to be getting in the hospital or skilled nursing facility. I mean simply that your voice is the voice your aging parent would want to raise if he or she could do it.

Admittedly, this chapter is rather "in your face." It has the tone of someone who knows how to be pushy, and I sincerely hope that I do not offend you in suggesting the things I suggest. Even if you have never been the outspoken type, I urge you to consider this: if you have a vulnerable elder who is not capable of protecting himself or herself, you may be the only one who can stop the worst things from happening to your parent.

When elders must depend on others for care, for managing insurance claims, and for the attention their conditions warrant, they are at risk. Medical claims that don't get paid lead to collection nightmares. Poor care, medical mistakes, and lack of attention in care facilities can lead to serious harm. Any responsible parent would likely "go to bat" for a child who needs that parent to speak up. My point is that our elders can become our responsibility too, just as our children were. We need to be ever watchful for their proper care, seeing that claims are paid, bills are straight, and that their needs are met as much as we are able to do so.

This is not to suggest that things go wrong with everything all the time. Fair payment for medical claims and proper handling of insurance payments happen more often than not. Quality care in hospitals and care facilities happens daily. However, sometimes things fall down, and when they do, this chapter is for you.

If you take anything from this chapter, it is the idea that it is up to you to help, and if you personally can't speak up, please find someone who can. The quality of our elders' lives and treatment can sometimes depend on it.

How to Stand Up for Your Elder in the Health Care System

Our health care system is perhaps the most complex of all systems in our American society. Doctors, other health care providers, insurers, pharmacies, equipment providers, and a string of related entities are enough to baffle even the sophisticated. Traditionally, our elders have been trusting of doctors and others related to their health care. However, we know that things go wrong. Human beings make up the system, and human beings make errors.

Our increasingly complex system of health care delivery is fragmented, making it less reliable. It can't necessarily be trusted.

The Institute of Medicine estimates that approximately 98,000 people die each year due to preventable medical errors. Our Federal and state governments attempt to address this problem with various kinds of regulations, but when your aging loved one is in a hospital or under medical care, you cannot necessarily count on everyone's compliance with regulations. What do we do when we are responsible for the care of an elder, and we realize that something isn't right with their health care, or the payment for health care?

Someone besides the one receiving care has to be paying attention. We cannot entirely prevent doctors, nurses, hospitals and insurers, including Medicare, from making mistakes, but we can watch out. We believe that by doing so, we can at least improve the chances of the ones we love. We need to get over the idea that those delivering health care to our elders (and ourselves) are to be completely trusted. Even the best people can make mistakes, be too tired to see something obvious, or have a lapse in judgment.

As consumers, we can ask questions. We can call it to the attention of the person in attendance that something seems to be wrong. We can insist on protections, which may be optional. We can accompany our loved ones to medical visits and while they are in the hospital. If we get the "brush-off," we can insist on going up the chain of authority, until we get satisfaction. We can change doctors. We can ask for information. We can appeal negative decisions by insurers not to pay legitimate medical charges. There is much we can do as consumers.

The culture of health care is not entirely conducive to this idea that we can question the authority of the health care provider or its agents. However, the alarming rate of preventable deaths is at least getting some attention. It is our hope in writing this chapter that we can encourage some consumers to speak up when it is appropriate to do so, and to get over fear of rocking the boat.

Questioning Medical Care

The Internet has done a great deal to begin to change the culture of health care that traditionally left the patient and patient's family in the dark. In the past, we were unable to know a condition, or what to do for it, unless the doctor chose to tell us. People now go to the Internet to answer their own questions about medical conditions, drugs, and treatment alternatives. Gone are the days when there was no easy way to do research about health care. This is positive, in that it levels the field of information more than before. However, our American culture is still deeply entrenched in the idea that "the doctor knows best." Often, that is still true, and physicians are usually deserving of respect. The doctor is an essential player on the health care team, but not the only one on the team. You're on it, too.

Not all doctors are created equal, and not all are good at communication. The pressures of medical practice, reduced income by declining pay for services from private insurance, Medicare and Medicaid, and bureaucracies in our hospitals make the job of the M.D. harder than ever. There is a nationwide nursing shortage, which is expected to grow worse. This makes health care delivery riskier. However, the health care provider is still obligated to provide quality care, regardless of how difficult it is to do so. Consumers who place themselves in the hands of health care providers have a right to expect that basic standards of care will be met, wherever they are delivered. They also have a right to expect that they will receive or be able to get information they need, about whatever aspect of the health care system they encounter. Insurance is one area in which questions arise, and answers can be hard to find.

Questioning Medicare Errors And Denials

With Medicare (and Medicaid), we are facing very complex governmental bureaucracies, which are not consumer friendly, though they purportedly intend to serve millions of beneficiaries in a friendly way. Most people get overwhelmed in trying to fix a problem that comes up. Errors arise from Medicare's failure to pay for services that Medicare is supposed to pay for, or from billing, in general.

How do we go about approaching Medicare when a problem comes up? There is no simple answer to trying to untangle a problem for your aging loved one when Medicare makes a mistake or wrongly denies a legitimate claim. However, appeals from incorrect denials of payment for bills from providers do exist. It is useful to be able to access information on the government's websites, and sometimes, if one is patient, the answers are actually available on the Medicare or state government's Medicaid website.

On its website, Medicare (www.medicare.gov) provides a description of the beneficiary's Appeals and Grievances rights.

The government also prints information about your right to appeal on the back of the notice that is mailed to you to explain what Medicare paid for and what it did not pay for. That document is called the *Explanation of Medicare Benefits or Medicare Summary Notice*. Where you suspect a wrongful denial of your loved one's benefits, start with an appeal of the denial. Follow the Medicare instructions to the letter. This must be done in writing. Forms are available for making an appeal on the website, or by requesting them through the toll-free telephone number.

Do not count on a flawless system. Medicare's websites are unfortunately confusing to many recipients of benefits. If you have a problem or question about your loved one's Medicare payments for medical care, we suggest attempting to use the website first. If that does not work, or if you do not have access to or comfort with using the Internet, consider the toll-free numbers provided. You are going to get numerous "voice prompts," which you must follow. You may have a long wait. Millions of Americans use the toll free numbers.

The best times to make calls are during non-peak hours, and late in the day or evening, rather than early in the morning. Be very patient, have the Medicare card number (Social Security number), date of birth, and address of your loved one ready, and accept that you may have to repeat your information and request more than once. If you are acting on behalf of a parent, and your parent has not given permission for Medicare to discuss confidential medical information with you, your parent or loved one will have to give that permission by phone or in writing. Otherwise, you will not be able to obtain any information except that which is publicly available, and it may not help you.

If your complaint is about Medicare failing to pay for a doctor's bill, you may need information from the doctor as to the service in question. Be sure that you understand what the service was before you contact Medicare. The doctor's office should provide an explanation to you of the service, if it is not clear from the billing itself.

If Medicare has denied payment for a legitimate claim and you are unable to get help by going to Medicare's website, or by calling the toll-free number, you may need to seek legal advice. If you are responsible for a low or moderate income elder who cannot afford the usual attorneys' fees, free legal aid may be available. A national referral website, LawHelp.org (www.LawHelp.org), helps low and moderate income people find free legal aid programs in their communities.

Search the website by state to locate a legal aid office nearest your elder. Another site, which may help if LawHelp.org does not list what you need, is FindLegalHelp.org, (www.FindLegalHelp.org). Talking to an attorney may help you and your elder find out more specifically what to do if a claim for payment is denied, and the attorney may represent you're elder in the appeal process if that is indicated.

Private Insurance Companies

What happens when you have an issue with your loved one's private, supplemental insurance? In dealing with private insurers, you will have an experience similar to dealing with a governmental entity, though it could be even more difficult. There are no rules about "customer service" in dealing with private insurers. Good customer service is not required by either the state or Federal government regulations over private insurers, and it shows.

Suppose you have a billing error or denial of a claim for payment from the supplemental insurer for a service received. Your elder cannot afford the costly co-payment. You must be prepared to spend a long time trying to sort out the problem. Supplemental insurance companies, which provide additional coverage for things not covered by Medicare, are not there to make you happy. They are profit-making entities and will deny any claim for any service they believe they do not have to cover. Getting past the resistance to address the question you raise will take persistence on your part. Allow plenty of time for any telephone contact. This is not the sort of thing you can do in a fifteen-minute coffee break from work. Expect to wait on hold. Expect that the first person with which you speak will not be able to help you, and ask to speak to a supervisor.

To be certain that your request to correct a problem is not ignored, put it in writing, identifying the claim or problem you have by the identification number the insurer provides for your loved one. Use the invoice number of the bill, which was denied, as well as your elder's Medicare number, Social Security number, date of birth, address, policy number, and group number on the insurance identification card. Mail it to the insurance company's claims address and be sure to keep a copy. Call to follow up. It is common for insurance companies to "lose" letters, claims, and bills. Consider that when it comes to dealing with private insurance companies, the telephone is not enough. Put everything in writing.

There is no fast way to untangle a wrongfully denied claim or incorrect payment from an insurer. If you feel overwhelmed, and you are ineffective in dealing with the problem, get help. Some social service agencies serving elders will help with these problems. Community service centers sometimes provide help with insurance questions and problems. A social worker may be more effective in addressing an error, as the social worker is likely to be accustomed to dealing with bureaucratic structure. Social workers and other resources are available to the public through your nearest Area Agency on Aging.

Seek legal help if no social services help is available. You have rights as a consumer and you are not powerless in the face of a bureaucracy. It takes time, persistence, and assertiveness to get problems fixed. The appeal process generally exists with private insurers also, although Medicare's appeal will differ from that of any private insurer. If your elder's claim is denied or you are advised that a supplemental insurer refused to pay its share of an existing bill for your elder, ask about the appeal process. Sometimes it is called a "review."

Typically, one must go through the appeal or review process before taking other legal action against a company. Taking legal action against a private insurance company will involve legal deadlines, and it is critical to get advice from a lawyer as to what legal deadlines apply to the matter you have. These deadlines to make claims, also called "statutes of limitations," are strict. If someone tries to make a claim after the deadline is past, the court will not hear such a case.

Sometimes, the denial of a claim can be life threatening. If a needed procedure, test, or treatment is denied by an insurer, and it is supposed to be covered by the policy of insurance, it is time to seek legal advice right away. When an insurer denies a legitimate claim of its own insured, it can be a matter of what lawyers call "bad faith," a legal term. Many large insurers have committed acts of bad faith in denial of legitimate claims, and some have had to pay large sums of money when juries have found that the bad faith violated the law and caused terrible harm.

It cannot hurt you to seek the advice of an attorney who specializes in handling bad faith claims against insurance companies if you have been denied a claim and suffered serious harm. For bad faith cases, most attorneys do not charge for their time to review the facts with you and to investigate to see if there is a case. Be advised, though, that this is a highly complex area of the law. Few cases have enough to them to make a bad faith claim against an insurer. Many attorneys who handle such claims do so on a "contingent fee" basis. That is, they take the case with the hope of success, and take their fees from a successful verdict or settlement. The consumer does not pay money up front. Some exceptions exist.

Some lawyers who work in this area of the law require that their clients pay certain costs of having a case, apart from the attorney's fees. Every case has costs, which are separate from attorney's fees for the work the attorney does. These start with investigation, and include filing fees for court, and many other expenses which must be paid out of pocket. The larger the case, the more substantial the costs. If you need to seek legal advice about what you believe is wrongful denial of a legitimate claim, be sure to find a lawyer who does this work for a living, and who specializes in insurance or bad faith claims.

Your local Bar Association in the county where you live may have a website which lists attorneys by specialty area. If you live in a small town, choose the nearest large city, and look for a website for the Bar Association for the county where the large city is located. Personal referrals from someone you know are a good start in searching for the right lawyer to help you. See the "How to Find a Good Lawyer" chapter for more information.

Dealing With Hospitals

If your elder is hospitalized, and you are concerned about the quality of care, you are not helpless to try to fix it. You can speak up. The premise here is that it is appropriate to do so when your gut tells you that something is not right. The best person to take on this job is a polite and assertive person who is willing to do it.

When someone is hospitalized, we often have to deal with fears that the elder will not survive, or will be impaired. We can feel confused and filled with conflicting emotions. We may be visiting from another area, and feel unfamiliar with the location. However, it is not completely safe to assume that just because your elder is in a hospital, he or she will always get the best of care. One's own feelings of discomfort may need to be put aside to protect your aging loved one. Hospitals are filled with layers of authority; from administrators to physicians, nurses, and other health care workers; as well as heads of departments throughout the facility. Getting satisfaction when you have a problem may involve dealing with more than one of these layers.

One of the most intimidating things about hospitals for most people who are patients in them is that everyone in a position of power seems to be very busy. They are busy. Hospitals can be extremely busy, but this is not an excuse for poor care. If you have a question about the care your elder is getting (or not getting), it is prudent to approach the Registered Nurse first. Every patient in the hospital will have a nurse somewhere who is in charge of the care. Nurses are typically caring individuals, but the degree of compassion they have and their ability to address patient and family concerns will vary among individuals.

In raising a question or voicing a complaint about care, be polite. What you see or assume may have an explanation, which could change your mind. You will be easier for the health care team to deal with if you start out your communication courteously, rather than in a demanding way. However, one may need to raise the degree of assertiveness if you do not get a response after your first or second attempt to get something changed or done.

Your loved one's Primary Care Physician is essential to keeping him or her safe in the hospital. The doctor may be the one who admitted your family member to the hospital, and who may be called upon to keep track of all the other doctors and staff who care for your relative. Seek help from the primary care doctor if things do not seem to be going along properly. Make that call if you have concerns. The doctor is the head of the team you are on and needs to be aware of your concerns.

The R.N. in charge of your loved one may be a staff nurse, whose job is to deliver patient care, or a nurse manager, who has some administrative responsibility for nursing assignments. Either of them should be able to answer your questions. Ask for a meeting, a conversation, or an opportunity to ask questions. There is every reason to expect that you will be given the time to get the information you want.

For example, if the intravenous line your loved one is getting is removed and you do not know why, you should be able to find out. If Dad tells you he is getting a new medicine and it makes him groggy all the time, you certainly have the right to find out what it is and if this apparent side effect or grogginess is something he has to put up with, or if another medicine that can do the job without grogginess is available.

Grogginess is dangerous. People sometimes fall because of this. Therefore, it is within his and your rights as a consumer to ask about it. The person to ask is the nurse, who is generally more available to you than the doctors. Many other instances in which it is proper to ask questions exist any time your loved one is hospitalized. Don't be shy. If this is just "not you," and you are fearful for your loved one's safety, consider using an advocate from outside the hospital. A friend can speak for you. A geriatric care manager can also be a wonderful resource for you. (See the "How to Find and Use a Care Manager" chapter.)

If you are unable to tell whether the person coming into your loved one's room is a registered nurse, an aide, or some other hospital worker, ask. Most employees in hospitals are required to wear name badges, which specify their licenses, or titles. If it is not clear, it is fine to ask the person who enters your loved one's room if he/she is the registered nurse caring for your loved one. If not, ask the name of the person to whom you need to speak and where to find that nurse.

Regardless of whom it is that you approach with a problem, keep a record of the complaint, by date and time. Note the name of the person to whom you are talking about the problem. Document the problem as you see it. Note the date you became aware of it, what you saw, and whom you told about it. Keep a ledger, if necessary, to help you remember the specifics. A small notebook for pocket or purse will do fine. Without it, details can be lost, and the effectiveness of complaining can also be lost or undermined.

The Chain Of Command

In acute care hospitals, meaning those that care for people with illnesses which require other than "custodial" or maintenance care, there is typically a charge nurse on each unit where patient care is given. The charge nurse has responsibility for making patient assignments for that shift and she or he is a person in authority. The charge nurse supervises the staff nurses, nurses' aides, and other workers on the unit. If you have not received a satisfactory response from asking the nurse who entered your loved one's room, approach the person in charge with the problem.

Acute care hospitals may also have someone in charge of the charge nurse. That person may be called a nurse manager, Head Nurse, or by another title. He or she may have administrative authority to make assignments to charge nurses on each unit of the hospital and to supervise the charge nurses.

Above the Head Nurse is a Director of Nursing. The Director typically does not do any direct patient care, but is an administrator of the nursing staff. The Director's job involves budget, staffing, regulations, and other duties. In smaller, rural hospitals, a Director of Nursing may also be the Head Nurse. The smaller the hospital, the fewer layers of personnel in charge.

If there is a problem with nursing care, and you have spoken to the charge nurse without success, you may need to move up the chain of command to the next in authority over the charge nurse. These titles vary in different institutions. However, it is typical of a hospital to have a chain of command and increasing levels of authority going up the chain. If you ask to speak to a person in charge of your aging loved one, and you do not get any satisfaction, you will need to move up the chain until you are able to find the person who will listen to and act on your concerns.

When you have a concern about patient care for your loved one, it is necessary to persist, and to ask for the right person in the chain of command. It can be frustrating to voice your concerns and feel that no one is doing anything about them. Keep asking for the next higher up person in the chain of command if you do not get satisfaction. As you do, voice any complaints or concerns in a calm, courteous voice. You are likely to get more attention and a better response if you do not come across as angry, outraged, or rude. No one likes to deal with a shouting, rude person, even if the person is making a good, valid point.

Some hospitals have patient advocates who can assist you. Some handle complaints through hospital employees called "risk managers." Find out who hears complaints in the institution where your loved one is being cared for.

If you have a complaint about patient care, a worry that your elder is not being looked after properly, or that your loved one is not getting what the doctor ordered, speak up. Physicians and nurses are human, and have faults. Hospitals are filled with demands on their caregivers. Workers are usually faced with unpredictable things going on all the time. Health care workers can be overwhelmed by emergencies, difficult patients, and shortages of staff, heavy work assignments, and their own emotions. They can forget their assignment, or get distracted from something they set out to do, and your loved one can suffer as a result. It is important to see yourself as an advocate for your loved one if he or she must be in a hospital.

Generally, all patients in a hospital need someone to watch out for them and to stand up for them if they are too weak or ill to stand up for themselves. An articulate physician once commented, "If you have to go to a hospital, take your bitchiest friend with you." To me, this meant that you need an advocate to be there to keep an eye on your loved one, an advocate who is unafraid to speak up when something does not look right.

Doctors and hospitals are intimidating to most people who do not work in the health care field. The doctors and other health care workers have the knowledge of what is going on. The patient does not necessarily have such knowledge. The people delivering health care have the power to write orders, have things done, give or withhold information, tell you what to do, and keep or release your loved one from their care. That is a lot of power compared to what the consumer has.

No wonder it is intimidating to be in their environment where it feels so foreign to the average person. They even speak a different language, "medicalese," filled with unfamiliar terms and words the layperson does not understand.

As intimidating as it may seem, it is important to know that the patient has a right to good care in their hands. The patient's friend or family member can stand up for the right to good care if the patient is unwilling or unable to do this. It involves asking for explanations of things you need to know. It involves insisting on someone to check out a problem, give a medication to relieve pain, or do what seems is obviously needed if it is not being done. Speaking up takes courage. If you are the shy type, ask for someone to help you. Help does exist in hospitals and other health care institutions.

Discharge Coordinators And Case Managers

A discharge coordinator is a hospital employee who assists the family and patient in a care facility to transition out of the facility to another place. Many are social workers, and all are familiar with community resources. Some are also called case managers. They can be excellent resources for you if you have questions about care. Typically they will know the physicians who work on your loved one's floor or unit in the hospital or care facility. Often, they help manage cases from a "logistical perspective" or from the point of view of coordinating among the different things that need to be done by different people caring for the patient. This coordinating person can be very helpful if you have a complaint. He or she can direct you to the correct place in the facility to be heard or solve a care problem.

Risk Managers

Many hospitals hire specially trained persons to serve patients and families of patients who have complaints or problems with care given in their hospitals. These individuals are called Risk Managers. Many are nurses. Some are nurse-attorneys. Some are administrators.

Their job is to attempt to placate those with complaints and avoid legal conflicts over care given in the hospital. In a sense, the Risk Manager is the "complaint department" when a mistake has occurred. Risk managers are accustomed to listening to people who are dissatisfied with the care received or lack of care received. They often work to fix the problem by communicating with the patient or family. They often cover all parts of a hospital, and know the head nurse, charge nurses, and others who are in a position to address a problem.

They serve the hospital by minimizing, where possible, the risk that someone will be angry about what happened in the hospital and will want to sue the doctor or the hospital and its employees. The Risk Manager can be a very helpful person to the family member of a patient in the hospital, as this person has a more objective point of view than the direct caregiver, and has an interest in resolving conflict. She or he has the ability to "do something" in many situations in which the patient or family of the hospitalized person feels helpless and upset about care. Sometimes "doing something" involves listening in a respectful way and acknowledging the problem.

If you are attempting to solve a problem about your aging loved one's care in a hospital and have gotten no satisfaction from the staff nurses or charge nurses or head nurse, consider asking if the hospital has a Risk Manager. If so, request to see that person as soon as practical to do so. You are likely to get the Risk Manager's attention by asking for a meeting with him or her. Complaints about care in hospitals can sometimes lead to legal disputes and lawsuits. Risk Managers are there to reduce the hospital's risk of being sued and to smooth over relations with patients and families when possible.

Human Resources

In a large, acute care hospital, the Human Resources Department may also be a place to take a complaint about care if you have approached the nurses and the primary care doctor without success, or if the doctor is unavailable and you want to get something done sooner rather than later. If your loved one is in an HMO facility (such as Kaiser), start with the office of Member Relations. This office may have the authority to handle a complaint and to work with you, much as a risk manager does.

Top Of The Chain Of Command

The Chief Executive Officer (CEO) of the hospital is at the top of the bureaucracy. He or she may answer to the Board of Directors, but is the highest authority working in the hospital. If all else fails, you can go to the top with your concerns about care your loved one is receiving. It may be difficult to gain access to this individual, as the layers of authority below the CEO have the effect of protecting him or her from direct contact with patients and families. However, no CEO is going to want a disgruntled patient or family. Letter writing can be effective. This is a route to explore if you are unable to find help for your serious concern about your loved one by any of the other means mentioned above.

Taking The Emotion Out Of Your Complaint

Most of us have experienced emotionally charged interactions in our lives. Anger, fear, and a sense of powerlessness can drive people to say and do things they later regret. We know, in hindsight, that when we are swept up in our emotions, it is hard to think clearly, and we may communicate poorly or in a harsh and ineffective way. If you have a complaint to bring up in a health care setting, it is a good idea to stop and plan out how you are going to present the problem before you say anything. Otherwise, the real and legitimate complaint you may have can get lost by being upset and coming across to those in charge as a "nut." We suggest the following approach if you believe that your elder is not getting proper care.

First, collect information. If, for example, your elder was supposed to start physical therapy on Monday, and it hasn't started by Wednesday, rather than coming in screaming at the charge nurse, ask about the doctor's order for physical therapy. "I understood from the doctor that my Mom was supposed to start physical therapy two days ago. Did the doctor change the order?" This approach may cause the nurse to look at the physician's order and find out if perhaps the failure to start treatment was a mistake, or perhaps the order was changed for some reason. You have a right to know. Your elder has a right to know.

Sometimes, hospitals have a way of making older persons confused and disoriented, and your elder may not be sure of what day it is. That is why it is good for the family member in charge to ask for your aging loved one, when you have a question.

The charge nurse is more likely to be willing to look at the chart to confirm the doctor's order if approached with courtesy, rather than in another way. The temptation may be to say something like, "What's wrong with you people? My mother is getting bad care here! How come she didn't get physical therapy? Don't you care what happens to her?" The angry, accusatory approach will automatically put the hospital staff on the defensive, and they may avoid you. You might not find out what happened for some time, or ever. A polite and even tone of voice could lead to a finding that the order had been overlooked, and that physical therapy will now get started today.

The health care system in a hospital simply will not be perfect in every way. One might even discover in this hypothetical situation that there was a reason why the start of physical therapy was delayed, and it is okay, but no one told you about the change. Any scenario is possible in health care. We suggest that one not assume the worst first. On the other hand, do not let shyness or fear of approaching someone in authority stop you, as you may be the only one available to speak up. The patient is more vulnerable than you are, and you owe it to your loved one to seek answers. It is important to keep a careful record of each person you speak to about a complaint with names, dates, times, and telephone numbers you call. This can improve accountability of those who are supposed to assist in these situations.

Getting Pushy

Some call being assertive "pushy." We call it speaking up from a position of strength. Many find this role uncomfortable. For others who are accustomed to dealing with work situations in which layers of authority are involved, the role may come more naturally. When you're loved one's welfare in a health care institution may be at stake, it is certainly time to get pushy when things are not going right. Long-term care facilities are examples of where many things can go wrong.

Let's say, for example, your elderly aunt is in a nursing home, and she is unable to walk on her own. She needs help to move around. You are helping her, rubbing her back. You notice that the skin on her bottom is open and that she has a sore at her tailbone. This is called a pressure ulcer, "decubitus" or a bedsore. It can be very dangerous. You mention it to the nurse. She assures you that it will be fine, they know about it. You come back the next day and it's worse. You politely mention to the nurse, again, that you are concerned about the bedsore. You get the same response as before, don't worry. They know about it and they're dealing with it.

You return a day or two or a week later. The bedsore is much bigger and you think it looks a lot worse. Is it time to get pushy? Absolutely! Your elder's health is at stake here. The bedsore can get infected, that can lead to other complications and infections. It is time to go up the chain of command, and also to contact the treating physician. Elders are vulnerable. They may be in pain, but are not in the habit of complaining. Bedsores are painful. The elder may be confused, or unable to speak because of dementia, strokes, or other conditions. Perhaps they are too shy to speak up and ask for themselves. It is up to you to see that the proper care is given for this kind of problem before it gets out of control.

How do you approach the chain of command? First, ask to speak to the person in charge of the nurse who has been so reassuring that everything is fine. Ask to speak to the charge nurse, head nurse, or director. Ask to speak to all three. Ask for the Risk Manager. Write a letter of complaint to the director of nursing or hospital administrator. Call the physician, and ask for an explanation of the proper treatment your aunt is supposed to be getting for the bedsore.

Some people think this is being a pest. But a pest is likely to get something done. A quiet person who takes the reassurance that "everything is fine" while watching a bedsore get worse with one's own eyes is truly letting an elder loved one down. We advocate becoming a "squeaky wheel" when it comes to protecting your aging loved one.

A word of warning is that some long term care facilities, also called nursing homes, are just plain dangerous. They do not mean to be. They suffer from staff shortages, poor payment from Medicare and Medicaid, incompetent administrators, and other problems. Most people in long-term care facilities want to give good care, but some are simply unable to deliver. If you find your elder in such a place, where many signs of trouble are all around you, take heed and do what you can to get your loved one moved to another facility.

Complaining and being a vigorous advocate for an elder in a dangerous nursing home will not fix the danger. It is beyond your control and may be beyond the control of the people who work in the facility. It may be a corporate policy around profit making that causes a nursing home to be dangerous. It may be impossible to find enough qualified nurse's aides in the area to give proper care for the salary the facility will pay. Whatever the reason, it may be up to you to look as far and wide as necessary to protect your loved one from the threat of unsafe care.

Do not accept the situation of dangerous care. Even the poorest Medicaid recipient has a right to basic safety in health care. Our most vulnerable elderly members of society require our protection to assure their safety in these unfortunately dangerous places. If it takes time to find another facility, be present as much as possible while your loved one waits for a bed in a different care facility. You must be the safety police.

Ten Tips for Standing Up for Your Elder in the Health Care System

1. If a mistake is made by Medicare, Medicaid or private insurance, and a legitimate bill is denied, seek a review or appeal in writing. Be persistent and patient.

2. Use the government's websites first, if you can, to find out how to appeal a decision by Medicare or Medicaid (CMS), which you believe is incorrect. If you call an 800 number, do so during evening hours.

3. Know that medical mistakes are, unfortunately, common in hospitals and be protective in watching over your loved one in a hospital or other care facility.

4. Speak up if you see something that doesn't seem right. Don't be shy. Ask questions about care you feel may be wrong.

5. If you speak up and are not satisfied, keep going. Ask to speak to the supervising nurse in a hospital, if the caregiving nurse is unable to help you.

6. Be aware that there is a chain of command in institutions, which deliver health care. Go up the chain until you get someone to listen to your concerns.

7. Ask to speak to the hospital Risk Manager, if your hospital has one, in the situation of serious concern and no response from the persons caring for your elder.

8. Get pushy if you have a concern that has not been answered and the problem is growing worse over time. Be the squeaky wheel.

9. Collect information before you open your mouth to complain. Ask basic questions before jumping to conclusions that the care your elder is getting may be wrong.

10. Always approach any complaint or concern about care in a polite and respectful way. Take the emotion out of your complaint and you stand a better chance of being heard and helped.

References

Medicare. http://www.Medicare.gov.

LawHelp.org. http://www.LawHelp.org.

FindLegalHelp.org. http://www.FindLegalHelp.org.

Resources

To learn more about *The Boomer's Guide for Aging Parents* book series, and other valuable resources, please visit our website at AgingParents.com.

The Boomer's Guide to Aging Parents book Series

How to Handle a Dangerous Older Driver

How to Choose a Home Care Worker

How to Understand the Pros and Cons of Assisted Living

How to Choose a Nursing Home

How to Find and Use a Care Manager

How to Handle Money for Aging Loved Ones

How to Handle Family Conflicts About Elders

How to Find a Good Lawyer for Mom or Dad

How to Stand Up For Your Elder in the Health Care System

Purchase *The Boomer's Guide to Aging Parents* book Series at AgingParents.com. (Individual books are also available for purchase at Http://www.AgingParents.com/products

Made in the USA
Lexington, KY
29 November 2009